In Print

Reading Business English

Rod Revell
& Simon Sweeney

CAMBRIDGE
UNIVERSITY PRESS

Published by the Press Syndicate of the University of Cambridge
The Pitt Building, Trumpington Street, Cambridge CB2 1RP
40 West 20th Street, New York, NY 10011, USA
10 Stamford Road, Oakleigh, Victoria 3166, Australia

First published 1993

Printed in Great Britain at
the University Press, Cambridge

ISBN 0 521 38303 X

Acknowledgements

The authors would especially like to thank the partners
of York Associates, and also Fred Dobson of Eurolectric,
Hull and Ken Gove of Turbine Repair Developments,
Coventry for assistance during the research for this
book.

We thank Peter Donovan of Cambridge University
Press for help during the exploratory phase of writing
and his colleague Will Capel whose detailed study of the
manuscript led to many apt criticisms and suggestions.
Thanks also to Andy Wilson, freelance editor.

The author and publishers are grateful to the
publishers who have given permission for the use of
copyright material identified in the text It has not been
possible to identify the sources of all the material used
and in such cases the publishers would welcome
information from copyright owners.

Reed Business Publishing Group for the articles and
extracts from International Management on pp. 3, 52,
55, 63-65 and 72. Akzo Chemicals for the report on p.
5. Communications International for the extract on p.
6. European Journal of Marketing for the extract on p.
8. Robert Hunt Picture Library for the photograph on
p. 9. The Economist for the articles on pp. 9 and 75-77.
Wordstar International Ltd for the extract from the
Wordstar Training Guide on p. 10. Reed Travel Group
for the articles from Executive Travel on pp. 11 and 61.
Macmillan Computer Publishing for the extracts from
Quickstart 1-2-3 on pp. 16-20. Marshall Editions Ltd
for the extracts from The Manager's Handbook on
pp21-30 and 38. The Gower Publishing Group for the
extracts from The Gower Handbook of Management on
pp 34-36, 87, 89 and 91. Which Computer for the
extracts and articles on pp. 41-43, 45-46 and 68-69.
Random House, Inc for the extract from Going
International on p. 51. Gulf Publishing Company for
the article from Managing Cultural Differences on pp.
56-57. Communications Management for the article on
p. 70. The Financial Times for the extracts on pp.78-79.
The Organisation for Economic Co-operation and
Development for the report on p. 81. Simon & Schuster
International Group for the extracts from Accounting
for Management Decisions on pp. 96-97 and 99-100.
Peter Collin Publishing Ltd for the extracts from the
English Business Dictionary on p. 94. Professional Sport
-Boris Becker

Contents

Teacher's Introduction

The aim of this book is to provide skills, strategies and vocabulary that will enable non-native speaker Business English readers to read published business reading material as efficiently as possible.

Efficiency, in this context, is putting the minimum amount of work and effort (reading the minimum amount of text) into extracting the maximum amount of information from a given text.

The need for improved reading techniques

This book aims to show how specific strategies can make the information in texts more accessible and the reading process more fluent. Many learners using this book may be efficient readers in their native language. Experience shows that the simple transfer of skills from native language to target language rarely occurs. Learners all too frequently read a foreign language text with a painstaking dedication to deciphering every word in a linear fashion, frequently spending more time looking in a dictionary than reading the text. The result is at best a highly imperfect translation, at worst frustration and incomprehension.

Learner profile

The book has been written for practising managers at all levels, and for those following courses of study that will lead to their becoming managers.

Source material

The texts used are all authentic. They are from textbooks, handbooks, journals, newspapers, manuals, company accounts, reports and contracts.

Level

The texts have been chosen and the exploitation material designed for learners at an intermediate level or above. However, low intermediate learners, if they follow the techniques suggested and do not read in more detail than the instructions recommend, should cope well with most tasks and most texts.

Using the book

The Twelve Units. *In Print* is not a course. The units are not formally graded though easier texts are at the beginning and more difficult ones are at the end of the book. The units need not, with one exception, be used in any given order. Nor is it necessary to study all of them. The exception is Unit 1. You should do this unit first. It introduces the core reading skills that are essential for processing text efficiently. These skills are taken up and practised in subsequent units.

Introduction to each unit. This establishes the theme and gives the learner a purpose for reading, which is generally returned to at the end of the unit, summarising information from the reading texts.

Vocabulary. The Introduction also has a list of Key Words. It is important to make sure that learners know what these mean before they move on to the main body of the unit. The first task in each unit offers a check on the comprehension of the Key Words. Make sure that learners are equipped with good dictionaries and that they get into the habit of checking associated lexis (word families, etc) when looking up a new word. At this stage and at the end of each unit, learners should make their own vocabulary notes with examples showing how the words are used (see *To the learner*).

Texts and Tasks. Each unit contains three texts on the unit's topic and a number of tasks associated with each of the texts. These generally practise the skills introduced in Unit 1 or aim to develop vocabulary. **It is important to make sure that learners do not read in greater detail than is necessary for the task**. Learners may achieve greater comprehension but they will not be reading efficiently.

Answers to the tasks. Answers are in the Answer Key (page 110). The symbol >M< indicates that the answers given are models or samples of what is possible.

Transfer. The Transfer section at the end of each unit ties together the various threads. Often it is suggested that the learner write a report or memo. In the classroom situation, the information required can easily and usefully be transferred to other skills, especially presentations, discussions and meetings.

To the learner

This is a self-study guide for learners using the book without a teacher.

Who is *In Print* for?

In Print has been written for business people and for learners on Business Studies courses whose first language is not English. The aim of the book is to show you the best way to read business texts in English and to increase your knowledge of general Business English words. The 'best way' of reading is the way that takes a minimum of time and hard work and gives exactly the information that is necessary, no more, no less.

Using *In Print*

The book is divided into twelve units. Eleven of these units are on different areas of business. The units are not too specialised – most business people will find them useful for their work, but it is not necessary to study all the units and they can be read in any order. The texts in the early units are generally easier than those in the later ones. But before you look at Units 2-12, it is most important that you study Unit 1 first. This unit will introduce many of the reading techniques that are used and practised in Units 2-12.

How to study a unit

Organisation of each unit. Each unit begins with an Introduction. This will give you a reason for reading the texts that follow. Units 2-12 also have a list of the most important words – Key Words – that you will need to understand when you study the unit (see Dictionary Use on the next page). There is then a vocabulary exercise based on the Key Words.

When you are sure you know the meaning of the Key Words, start on the first of the three texts that each unit contains. Each text has a number of tasks or exercises with it. The tasks are based on reading techniques or vocabulary study. Follow the instructions carefully: don't read the text in more detail than the instructions tell you to. In several units there are opportunities to include ideas based on your own studies, work and experience.

Each unit ends with a Transfer activity usually designed to summarise information from the texts in each unit. This often includes the option of writing a short report or memo. The Transfer activity frequently includes an opportunity to use ideas based on your own studies, work and experience (for examples, see units 2, 3, 4, 5, 9, 10, 11).

Answer Key. The answers to the tasks are in the Answer Key (page 110). When you see >M< in the key, the answer in the key is one of a number of different possible answers.

Timing for each unit. It is not possible to say exactly how much time you will need for each unit. This will depend on your knowledge of English and the way in which you learn. Work at the speed that is best for you. As a general guide, each unit should take between 3 and 4 hours. Do not spend too long on any task or unit.

Dictionary use. Always have good general and business dictionaries with you when you use a book. They can be English-English or English-your language, or both. The best sort of dictionary is the bigger one that gives you examples of how to use words. See for example The Longman Active Study Dictionary, The Oxford Advanced Learner's Dictionary, The Longman Dictionary of Contemporary English or Collins COBUILD English Language Dictionary. When you look up the meaning of words, always check for other words in the same word family (see Unit 3, Task 8).
Use the dictionary to check the meaning of any key words you do not know. Take care to select the right part of speech, normally indicated by *n* (noun), *v* (verb), *adj* (adjective), etc. Even more importantly, select the right meaning if there are various alternatives. Usually these are numbered 1, 2, 3, etc in the dictionary. Study the examples given in the dictionary to make sure you understand the word in different contexts.
When studying the texts, do not use the dictionary automatically for every word you do not know. Use the dictionary only if:
i. you decide a word is especially important; and

ii. you cannot guess its meaning from the context (see Unit 1 Technique 7, Task 9).

Making vocabulary notes. This book will teach you a lot of new words. Create your own vocabulary list based on the words you learn from the book. You should note any words you look up in the dictionary. Make sure that you write information about how the word is used. Note if it is a noun (*n*), adjective (*adj*) or adverb (*adv*), etc. If it is a verb, always include the infinitive particle *to,* and note if it is used with a particular preposition. Also note if there are related words. Finally include example sentences. Here is a model vocabulary note:

> to compete/to compete with s.o.
> competition (*n*) competitive (*adj*)
> We have to compete with cheap imports.
> The competition in the video camera market is very strong.

Include any other useful information, such as details of irregular verbs. Making vocabulary notes like this takes time and should be a separate study activity from reading the texts. The best time for making vocabulary notes (and for extended use of the dictionary) is during your study of the Key Word lists, while doing the vocabulary related tasks, or when you have finished a unit of *In Print*. This will be a useful part of your studies, and you will also create a personalised store of vocabulary for future reference.

Introductory Unit

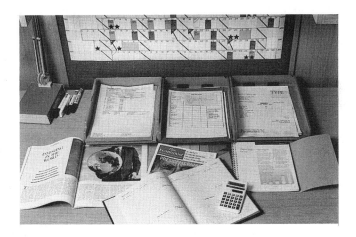

Introduction

In business, many kinds of text arrive on desks every day. Look at the illustration above. What kinds of text can you identify? What other kinds of reading material could be included?

There is never enough time to read everything. The objective of this book is to help you to read better. This does not mean simply reading more quickly. It means spending a minimum of time getting maximum understanding from what you read.

INPUT		OUTPUT
Reading time	⟶	Understanding
(Minimum)		(Maximum)

Keep a positive view. You must want to improve your reading. Read as much as possible in English and try to follow the techniques explained and practised in this book.

This unit contains examples of some of the reading activities in the book. First, we look at some words that will help you to use this and other units in the book.

Using this book (or any other book or magazine) find examples of the following:

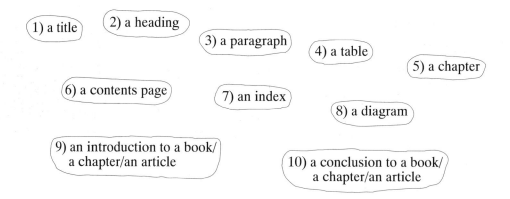

1) a title
2) a heading
3) a paragraph
4) a table
5) a chapter
6) a contents page
7) an index
8) a diagram
9) an introduction to a book/ a chapter/an article
10) a conclusion to a book/ a chapter/an article

Technique 1: Scanning for specific information

Task 2

You work for a Management Training organisation. One course you offer is about Industry and Pollution. The following text is part of the Contents page from the magazine *International Management*, and one article could be useful for your course. Find the title of the article and its page number.

CONTENTS

January 1989 Vol. 44 No. 1

Now let's examine how you decided which article you would read:

- Did you read *every word* to decide what to read?
- What were the words that indicated articles of interest?
- Which picture was important?

If you decided in only a few seconds that the article on page 24 was the right article to read, then you used the correct reading technique. We can call this **Scanning for specific information**. The words 'environment' and 'green' and perhaps 'company' in the title of the article and the picture of the dying trees tell you which is the relevant article. It was not, of course, necessary to read every word on the page, or even the description of the article.

When you scan a page or an article, it is not necessary to read everything to find what is of special interest to you. Look for words, pictures, etc., which indicate what you need to know. This is scanning.

Task 3

The same scanning technique can be used with the following text, which is a half yearly report for 1986 from the Dutch chemicals company Akzo.

Scan the text to find information about whether sales went up or down in the product areas given below. Then say why the changes happened. The first answer is given as an example.

Product Area	Result	Reason
Man-made fibres	Sales down[1]	Divestiture of American Enka[2]
Pharmaceuticals		
Consumer products		

[1] See underlined words in the text or sales table at the bottom of the text.

[2] See underlined words in the text.

Where did you look for this information? Notice the importance of typeface, i.e. the product areas mentioned in the text (e.g. *Pharmaceuticals*) are easily identifiable by the *italics*.

4

Akzo

Consolidated statement of income

		1st half year	
		1986	**1985**
Net sales	Millions of guilders	8,092.7	9,164.8
Operating income		728.2	744.4
Financing charges		(60.9)	(108.9)
Operating income less financing charges		667.3	635.5
Taxes on operating income less financial charges		(226.9)	(225.7)
Earnings of consolidated companies from normal operations, after taxes		440.4	409.8
Earnings from nonconsolidated companies		17.4	56.9
Extraordinary items		24.1	34.6
Group income		481.9	501.3
Minority interest		(45.2)	(42.0)
Net income		436.7	459.3
Net income per common share of Hf l20, in guilders		10.92	11.55
Common stock		799.9	795.1

Sales and income

Sales for the first six months of 1986 aggregated Hfl 8.1 billion, down 12% from the first half of 1985. Divestitures and acquisitions account for a 6% decrease, with translation of the sales of foreign Group companies at lower rates of exchange accounting for another 5% drop.

After-tax earnings of consolidated companies from normal operations increased 7% compared with the first half of 1985 and amounted to Hfl 440 million.

Earnings from nonconsolidated companies was adversely affected by lower results of the fiber companies in Latin America and India. The start-up cost of the aramid plants was also charged against income.

The positive balance of extraordinary items in the first half of 1986 is principally due to deferred revenue from the 1983 sale of Brand-Rex (Akzo America).

Compared with the first half of 1985 net income fell 5% to Hfl 437 million, corresponding to Hfl 10.92 per share (1985: Hfl 11.55). Before extraordinary items the drop in net income compared with 1985 was 3%.

1 The sales decline for *man-made fibers* is for the most part 2 attributable to the divestiture of American Enka. This divestiture caused operating income for the first six months to improve from 6.0% of sales in 1985 to 9.1% in 1986. Textile and carpet fibers continued their improved development. Industrial fibers are under increasing competitive pressure.

The dip in sales of *chemical products* is substantially due to the lower rate of the U.S. dollar. For most chemical products capacity utilization was high. Margins for specialty chemicals were slightly above the 1985 level. Starting from the second quarter the figures include the results of the recently acquired Perchem group (U.K.).

The advance in sales of *coatings* is due to companies acquired in 1985. The weather-induced first-quarter lag for some products was made up in the second quarter. Earnings in a few product sectors continued depressed.

Pharmaceuticals sales were up as a result of acquisitions made in 1985. The decrease in operating income was almost entirely due to the adverse effects of changed rates of exchange, which could not be sufficiently compensated by price adjustments because of government-imposed price controls.

Lower sales of *consumer products* reflect the divestiture of Romi (oils and fats) at January 1, 1986. Overall, profit margins were distinctly better in the second quarter of 1986 than in the first, boosting operating income for the first six months to a level slightly above that of the prior-year period.

In *miscellaneous products*, the sales gain was due in part to the acquisition of Wilson Fiberfil (engineering plastics). Barmag AG's performance continued strong in the second quarter of 1986. Results of the other products are under downward pressure, so that earnings for the entire class of miscellaneous products were virtually unchanged.

The equity/debt ratio at June 30, 1986 worked out at 0.66, against 0.62 at December 31, 1985.

Outlook

There is no change in our projection that net income for the whole of 1986 will be in the order of the 1985 figure. But this projection is subject to the qualification that oil prices and exchange rates remain unpredictable and could have a major impact on earnings.

Arnhem, August 1986   The Board of Management

The breakdown of sales and operating income by product group was as follows (in millions of guilders):

Sales	1st half year		Operating Income	1st half year	
	1986	**1985**		**1986**	**1985**
Man-made fibers	1,853	2,739	Man-made fibers	168	165
Chemical products	2,284	2,716	Chemical products	223	251
Coatings	1,162	1,051	Coatings	66	63
Pharmaceuticals	1,144	1,042	Pharmaceuticals	163	173
Consumer products	730	861	Consumer products	50	49
Miscellaneous products	1,057	898	Miscellaneous products	74	76
	8,230	9,307		744	777
Intra-Group deliveries	(137)	(142)	Not allocated	(16)	(33)
Total	8,093	9,165	Total	728	744

Technique 2: Predicting what is and what is not in a text

Now we look at an example of the use of the title and headings to help us to understand what is and what is not in an article. This is important because by understanding the title we can begin to think about what information we will find in the text and where we will find it. From the extracts below – title, some bold introductory text and some headings – we can see that certain themes or topics will be discussed in the articles.

The extracts are from an article in the journal *Telecommunications International*. Match 1 – 5 in the illustration below with the following themes. Sometimes more than one answer is possible.

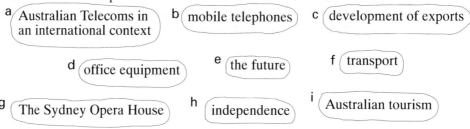

a Australian Telecoms in an international context
b mobile telephones
c development of exports

d office equipment
e the future
f transport

g The Sydney Opera House
h independence
i Australian tourism

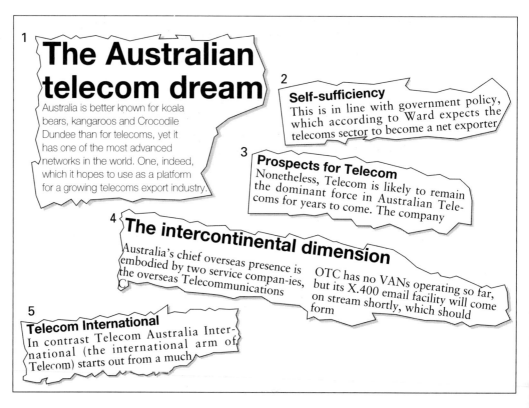

1 **The Australian telecom dream**
Australia is better known for koala bears, kangaroos and Crocodile Dundee than for telecoms, yet it has one of the most advanced networks in the world. One, indeed, which it hopes to use as a platform for a growing telecoms export industry.

2 **Self-sufficiency**
This is in line with government policy, which according to Ward expects the telecoms sector to become a net exporter

3 **Prospects for Telecom**
Nonetheless, Telecom is likely to remain the dominant force in Australian Telecoms for years to come. The company

4 **The intercontinental dimension**
Australia's chief overseas presence is embodied by two service compan-ies, the overseas Telecommunications C   OTC has no VANs operating so far, but its X.400 email facility will come on stream shortly, which should form

5 **Telecom International**
In contrast Telecom Australia International (the international arm of Telecom) starts out from a much

Task 4 has practised the technique of looking at an article and seeing what information you can find. Of course, as you do this, you also learn what you will not find in the article. When you have selected something to read, first look at the title, the headings and any bold text. Look at the length and any pictures or graphic material, eg. diagrams, tables, etc. Then ask yourself 'What will the article tell me?' or 'What information is probably in this article?' This is prediction.

Technique 3: Identification of the main points in a text

One way of identifying the main points in a text is to read only the first one or two paragraphs and the last one or two. This is especially the case in long articles where you may see the words Introduction, Summary or Conclusion. **Do not read the whole text in detail at this stage**. Read only the Introduction, or the first paragraph carefully. Then read the final part of the text or the last two paragraphs. We can call this part of a 'beginning/end principle'. The beginning and the end of long texts often have the most important information.

Task 5

On the next page are extracts from a report published in the *European Journal of Marketing*. Read the extracts and decide which of the following statements are true and which are false.

1 The United States imports many cars.
2 The number of imported cars in the US is going down.
3 There is no information about US attitudes to Japanese cars.
4 Understanding consumer attitudes is not important.
5 US attitudes to European cars are positive.

Here are the first two paragraphs of the report.

Attitudes Towards European, Japanese and US Cars
by Jacqueline J. Brown, C. David Light and Gregory M. Gazda
University of San Diego

The United States is one of the most important marketplaces for cars in the world. This is due not only to the size of its market, but also to the discretionary income of its consumers. During the last 15 years, foreign cars have been imported into the United States in increasing numbers and currently account for approximately 26 per cent of total US car sales.

It is commonly accepted that consumers' attitudes influence their buying decisions. However, what attitudes do US consumers hold about cars produced in various countries? Better understanding of these attitudes would be helpful in developing more effective marketing strategies for car manufacturers exporting cars to the United States. The purpose of this study is to evaluate and compare US consumer attitudes towards cars produced in four European countries (West Germany, England, France and Yugoslavia), Japan, and the United States and to suggest strategies for marketing foreign cars in the US.

The report has a final section headed 'Conclusion and Recommendations'. Here are the first and last paragraphs of this section.

Conclusion and Recommendations

Designing an effective marketing strategy for today's international market is becoming increasingly difficult. Factors such as country-of-origin biases, which are not significant in domestic competition, must be carefully considered in the international marketplace. Awareness and understanding of US consumers' attitudes towards foreign products can help in designing more effective product, price, promotion, and distribution strategies.

As the results of this study suggest, US consumers possess a very favourable image of a car manufactured in Germany and positive images of cars produced in France and England. These facts should provide European car manufacturers with some satisfaction and significant strategic marketing considerations. The "European car" image is a positive one; and strategically employed, it could become the basis for a distinct competitive advantage as car manufacturing and marketing become ever more global.

Identify the main point of the whole report.

Technique 4: Skimming to identify the main points in each paragraph

Skimming is reading quickly, without attention to detail, with no special attention to unknown words. The objective of skimming is to identify quickly the main points in each paragraph. It is often not necessary to understand everything in a paragraph to understand the main points.

Task 6

Skim the following article on the market for saxophones, taken from *The Economist*. In the first three paragraphs, the main points are underlined. Select what you think are the main points in paragraphs d, e and f.

Blowing a sweet horn

Paris

a) <u>SELMER</u> is to the saxophone as Stradivarius or Guarneri are to the violin. For jazzmen, there is none better – and jazz is back in fashion. The 103-year-old family firm also makes woodwinds, brass instruments and accessories, but 55% of Selmer's turnover of FFr130m ($22m) in 1987 came from its <u>saxophones</u>.

(b) In the <u>1970s Selmer hit unaccustomed trouble</u> from its choosy clientele and from Japanese competitors. For a period, Selmer risked losing its single greatest asset: word-of-mouth in the trade that Selmer was top.

(c) Between 1954 and 1973, when Selmer sold 150,000 Mark VI tenor saxophones, the instrument became a jazz legend. Feeling (it's not clear why) a need to innovate, Selmer in 1973 brought out a new model, the Mark VII. It never caught on. Small changes to a sax's keys can mean a player re-learning fingerings that took years to master. <u>Jazzmen</u> complained of small technical faults in the Mark VII and disliked its tone. Many <u>preferred</u> to buy second-hand Mark VI's out of hock, or worse, to buy a <u>Japanese instrument.</u>

(d) In the late 1960s Yamaha, a Japanese company, had begun selling high-quality saxophones closely modelled on Selmer's and whose pitch, even Selmer admits, "may have been truer than ours". The real snag was that Yamaha's were a third to a fifth cheaper.

(e) Selmer quickly retired its Edsel of saxophones and in 1981 brought out a new tenor, the Super-Action 80. Some professionals even prefer this now to the legendary Mark VI. Backed by their testimonials, Selmer has been able to take full advantage of a boom in jazz courses in American universities. But, especially with all those cherished second-hand Selmers competing with their own new instruments, Selmer may be reaching a limit in the American market. It has therefore put a big sales effort into opening up markets outside America. Japan now accounts for 20% of its total sales.

(f) Labour cost is a big worry. The Selmer factory at Mantes just outside Paris is an odd mixture of craftshop and assembly line. To keep up with robotised Yamaha, Selmer has had to streamline production. Yet many of its 50 workers, who belong to the same union-branch as Renault's or Peugeot's carworkers, do routine manual tasks: banging out the two halves of a saxophone bell or shaving cane to make reeds. Thirty years ago, Selmer used to say, "A saxophone is two kilos of brass and 60 hours of hard work." The instrument still weighs the same. But it takes close to a third as long to make.

More choices for Roland Kirk.

Technique 5 Prediction: What's coming next in the text?

Technique 2 looked at how headings and bold type indicate what information is in a text. Specific words or a particular phrase (part of a sentence) can also help us to predict what is coming next. They signal what is coming. Examples are phrases like **'The first thing to do is'** ... , **'Secondly'** ... , **'The last stage is'** ... . Recognising and understanding signalling words and phrases can help you to read more efficiently. They also help you to understand the structure of the text. Task 7 practises this technique.

Task 7

The texts below are two extracts from a manual for a Sanyo Word Processor. Look at the first extract and find words or phrases which:

1 indicate that the next sentence probably gives examples of differences.
2 here mean 'for example'.
3 indicate a sequential relationship.

Word Processing Methods

Even though you will be using a keyboard that looks very much like a typewriter keyboard, there are some major differences between typing on a typewriter and using WordStar. To begin with, the words you enter using WordStar are not immediately printed on paper. First, they are stored in the computer's memory (what you see on the screen is an image from one small segment of computer memory). Then, after you have completed your document, you save it on one of your diskettes. Finally, after you have decided to print your document, you print it from your diskette.

Now look at the second extract and decide which word or words are used to indicate the following:

4 a difference between two things.
5 an example.
6 something you will do later.
7 something you can think about now.

The Screen

The typing you do at your keyboard will appear first on a video screen, not on a sheet of paper. But unlike a sheet of paper, your screen will give you helpful information. For example, after you start typing, it will tell you the name of your file, your current page, line, and column in the file, and prompts to help you along. In the next lesson you will get your first chance to look at an actual screen display. For now, it should be enough to mention that the screen shows you information displays, error messages, and the text you are typing. To help you find your place, you will find a special character called the cursor at the location on the screen where you will type next

---

Technique 6 Reference: Understanding the relationship between sentences

This technique is closely related to Technique 5. The following article, from the magazine *Executive Travel*, contains many words which refer to other words in the same text. This gives the article an internal structure.

Task 8

First, skim the text and find the most important news (information) in the text. Do not use a dictionary.

Now, in the first paragraph, the words in bold in line 1 refer to the word(s) underlined in line 3. Note that the second example in bold in lines 2&3, refers to words underlined in the **next** paragraph. In paragraphs 2 and 3, other words in bold are marked [a], [b] and [c]. Say what they refer to.

Runway warning

A grim warning that by the end of the century an estimated **20 million passengers** using **London's two principal airports** will be diverted or grounded has provoked a sharp reaction from the Air Transport User's

5   Committee.

Commenting on a Civil Aviation Authority document on the future of air traffic, **the passenger watchdog body**[a] says that additional runway capacity is needed now at both Heathrow and Gatwick airports.

10   It points out that much of the diverted traffic is likely to go to **Continental hubs**[b], such as Schiphol or Charles de Gaulle, **the latter of which**[c] is planning a five runway airport handling 90 million passengers a year.

'A fifth terminal at Heathrow and a second at Stansted
15   seem certain to be necessary and inevitable', says the ATUC. 'But without more runways where they are wanted – at Heathrow and Gatwick – the inconvenience to users and economic cost to the nation escalate rapidly,' it adds.

Technique 7 Vocabulary: Predicting the meaning of a word from the context

Using a dictionary to find out the meaning of every word you do not know takes too long and reduces the efficiency of your reading. It is important to attempt to guess the meaning of words that you do not know. Usually, the context (the rest of the text and especially words and sentences close to the unfamiliar words) will help you to decide on a possible meaning for them.

Task 9

Look again at the text 'Runway warning'. Decide which definition is the closest to the meaning of the given word as used in the text.

1 grim (line 1)   a) very serious
                       b) short
                       c) angry

2 grounded (line 3)   a) delayed
                       b) mechanically disabled
                       c) not able to take off

3 hubs (line 11)   a) capital cities
                       b) city airports
                       c) important centres

4 escalate (line 18)   a) get worse
                       b) increase
                       c) decrease

Only look up a word in a dictionary if you have no idea what it means and you are confident that it is necessary to understand the word to get the information you need.

Other recommendations when reading long texts:

Use Contents pages, indexes, lists of tables, etc., to locate parts of a book, manual or report that are of special interest.

Do not fix your eyes on every word. You should let your eyes move over the text at a constant speed, looking at several words together.

Do not read aloud. Reading aloud is a separate skill, useful for practising pronunciation and as part of the preparation for giving presentations.

Do not read the same sentence or paragraph again and again. Disregard any part that is of no interest or is impossible to understand. However, you can of course spend more time on parts, or paragraphs of special interest.

Summary of the terms *Scanning* and *Skimming*

To scan (v). To look briefly at a text before reading it to see if (or where) it contains specific information that you are looking for. When you find the information you want, you read that section in more detail.

Examples:
• Scanning a train timetable to find out a departure time.
• Scanning a newspaper Contents list to find the page number for the financial news.
• Scanning an annual report to find the paragraph dealing with one particular product.

To skim (v). To read a text without attention to detail but looking only for main ideas. This will include attention to title, headings, introduction and conclusion, as well as main points in paragraphs. In skimming a text, it is not necessary to read every word.

Examples:
• Briefly looking at a newspaper to understand the main points of the news.
• Reading a 20 page report in 10 minutes to get the key ideas.
• Reading only the headings, the introduction, conclusion, or a summary of a report, and looking at pictures, graphs, etc.

Here is a basic method for reading long texts.

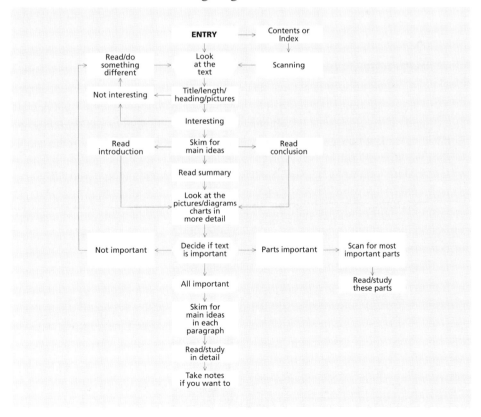

Business Software

Introduction

You have recently decided to do all your financial planning and reporting on your personal computer. To make this possible, you plan to use the Lotus 1-2-3 software and have bought the book *1-2-3 Quick Start*.

Many common English words have been incorporated into computer-related language. Most of the following words are examples of this. Task 1 is based on meanings related to computing. Study the list of words, do Task 1, then look up any words you do not know in a good dictionary.

Key Words

application	logo	graph
command	to manipulate	graphics
coordinate	menu	grid
to delete	password	to scroll
directory	prompt	spreadsheet
file	rectangle	
framework	to retrieve	

Explain the meaning of the underlined words in the sentences below. Give alternative words in English.

1 A common <u>application</u> of <u>spreadsheet</u> software is studying company accounts.
2 The <u>command</u> ∧BU (Control B, then U) underlines text.
3 The main <u>menu</u> appears when you enter Lotus 1-2-3.
4 To access the database enter your username then your <u>password</u>.
5 If you make a mistake, <u>delete</u> the characters you have entered using the backspace delete key (↵).
6 When you have entered the program, a dollar <u>prompt</u> ($) will appear on the screen.
7 Check the <u>directory</u> to see if the <u>file</u> has been saved.
8 If you delete a file by mistake, you can <u>retrieve</u> it from the system memory. This is not possible if you have logged out.
9 The software has sophisticated <u>graphics</u> capabilities. You can create complex charts, diagrams, tables and <u>graphs</u>.
10 The database offers you several options. <u>Scroll</u> the options by pressing the spacebar.

Text 1

Pre-reading

Task 2

Lotus 1-2-3 is an electronic spreadsheet program. In the left hand column below is a list of what is used, and what is done, when financial work is done in the traditional way. Which parts of the electronic spreadsheet technique (listed on the right) correspond to each item?

1 piece of paper   a) computer processor
2 pencil   b) keying in data columns
3 calculator   c) adding new data means
4 writing data by hand   automatic updating
5 adding new data means   d) screen
   rewriting everything   e) keyboard and cursor

Task 3

Scan the description of Lotus 1-2-3 on the next page and decide which of the following it can produce:

1 financial spreadsheets   3 financial reports
2 database applications   4 graphs

The Lotus 1-2-3 Electronic Spreadsheet

The electronic spreadsheet is the foundation of the 1-2-3 program. The framework of this spreadsheet contains the graphics and data-management elements of the program. You produce graphics through the use of spreadsheet commands. Data management occurs in the standard row-column spreadsheet layout.

What are the conventions that make 1-2-3 an excellent spreadsheet program? Firstly, 1-2-3 is designed as an electronic replacement for the accountant's columnar pad, pencil and calculator. Secondly, 1-2-3 understands relationships among all of the numbers and formulae in a single application and automatically updates values whenever a change occurs. Thirdly, 1-2-3's commands simplify and automate all the procedures related to creating, changing, updating, printing, and graphing spreadsheet data.

Task 4

Which of the four sentences on the page opposite match each of the screens below?

1

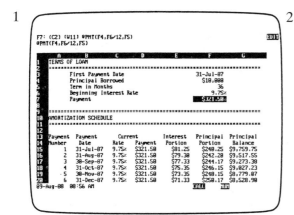

2

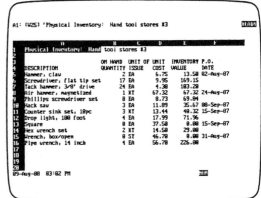

3

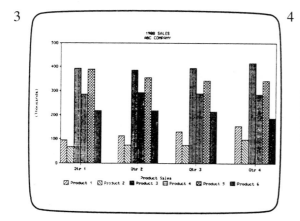

4

a With the database features of 1-2-3, you can manage and manipulate data, using 1-2-3's commands and database statistical functions.

b Using 1-2-3's macros and command language, you can automate and customise 1-2-3 for your particular application.

c 1-2-3's electronic spreadsheet replaces traditional financial modelling tools, reducing the time and effort required to perform even sophisticated accounting tasks.

d 1-2-3's graphic capabilities let you create five different graph types.

Task 5

Read this text on the key Lotus 1-2-3 concepts and then complete the spaces in the sentences which follow.

Key Lotus 1-2-3 concepts

Each row in 1-2-3 is assigned a number and each column is assigned a letter. The intersections of the rows and columns are called cells. Cells are identified by their row-column coordinates. For example, the cell located at the intersection of column A and row 15 is called A15. Cells can be filled with three kinds of information: numbers, mathematical formulae, including special spreadsheet functions and text (or labels).

A cell pointer allows you to write information into the cells as much as a pencil lets you write on a piece of paper. In 1-2-3, as in most spreadsheets, the cell pointer looks like a bright rectangle on the computer's screen. The cell pointer typically is one row high and one column wide.

With 8,192 rows and 256 columns, the 1-2-3 worksheet contains more than 2,000,000 cells. Each column is assigned a letter value ranging from A for the first column to V for the last. A good way to visualise the worksheet is as one giant sheet of grid paper that is about 7 m (21 feet) wide and 53 m (171 feet) high!

Because the 1-2-3 grid is so large, you cannot view the entire spreadsheet on the screen at one time. The screen thus serves as a window onto the worksheet. To view other parts of the sheet, you scroll the cell pointer across and down (or up) the worksheet with the arrow keys. When the cell pointer reaches the edge of the current window, the window begins to shift to follow the cell pointer across and down (or up) the spreadsheet.

---

1 The 1-2-3 spreadsheet contains 8,192 (a) . . . .

   and 256 (b) . . . .

2 A (c) . . . . is the intersection of a column and a row.

3 The (d) . . . . is the highlighted rectangle that

   allows you to enter data into the spreadsheet.

4 The screen serves as a (e) . . . . onto the worksheet.

5 To view other parts of the screen, you (f) . . . . the cell

   pointer across and down (or up) the worksheet.

Text 2

Read the instructions for starting 1-2-3 on a hard disk system first, then put in the correct order the instructions for starting 1-2-3 on a floppy system.

Starting Lotus 1-2-3

Starting 1-2-3 from DOS requires several steps. (We're assuming that the 1-2-3 program is on your hard disk in a sub-directory named 1-2-3.) Start 1-2-3 on a hard disk system as follows:

1 With the C> system prompt displayed on your screen, change to the 1-2-3 directory by typing CD/1-2-3 and pressing Enter.
2 Start 1-2-3 by typing 1-2-3 and pressing Enter.

Start 1-2-3 on a floppy system as follows:

1 **a**. If the a> prompt is not displayed, type A: and press Enter.
2 **b**. Start 1-2-3 by typing 1-2-3 at the A> system prompt, and press Enter.
3 **c**. After booting your computer with your DOS disk, remove the DOS disk and place the 1-2-3 System disk into drive A. After a few seconds, the 1-2-3 logo appears. The logo remains onscreen for a few seconds; then the worksheet is displayed, and you're ready to use 1-2-3.

Now read how to exit from 1-2-3.

To exit 1-2-3, you use the 1-2-3 main command menu. To access the menu, press the slash (/) key. The two commands you'll use to return to DOS from 1-2-3 are /**S**ystem and /**Q**uit.

Using /System To Exit 1-2-3
/System returns you to the DOS system prompt but does not exit the 1-2-3 program. You can perform system operations at the DOS level, including changing directories and drives, and then return to the 1-2-3 spreadsheet by typing **exit**. To select the **S**ystem option, type **S** or use the pointer to highlight the selection.
You'll find that /**S**ystem is a useful command when you need to check the amount of memory you have on disk before you copy a file to it or when you want to see how much memory a particular spreadsheet uses before you load it. /System saves you the trouble of having to quit the 1-2-3 program, issue the appropriate DOS commands, and then get back into the spreadsheet.

Using /Quit To Exit 1-2-3
/**Q**uit, also available on the 1-2-3 main menu, allows you to exit the worksheet and the 1-2-3 program. You are asking to verify this choice before you exit 1-2-3 because your data will be lost if you quit 1-2-3 without saving your file. To verify that you want to exit, type **Y** or move the pointer to **yes** and press **enter**.

Text 3

Pre-reading

Task 7

Check the meanings of these words by writing them in the correct place in the
following sentences: cursor/disk/file/display/enter/menu/select

---

To use /File Save

(a)..................... the 1-2-3- main (b)..................... by typing /.
(c)..................... file by positioning the (d)................... on that item or by typing **f**.
(Press enter if you have selected the command by moving the (d).....................).
Choose **S**ave or press **s**.
(e)................. a (f)................. name that you haven't used before; one
that in some way identifies the (f)............... so that you will be able to find it later.
Press Enter, and the file is saved to (g).................

Task 8

Look at the screens below and the texts on the following page and use them to help
you order the steps for password protecting a worksheet.

1
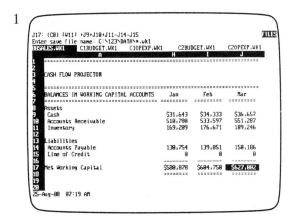

2
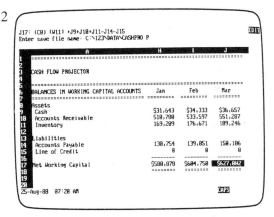

3
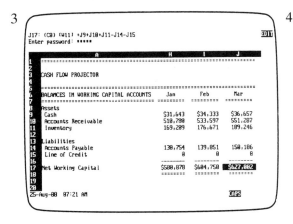

4
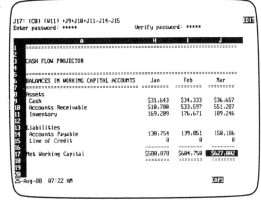

Task 9

Read the text below and then write instructions for each of the part screens underneath it.

You can delete a password by retrieving the file with the password you want to delete. Then, when you are ready to save the file, select the /**Fi**le **S**ave command. When the prompt appears, erase (PASSWORD PROTECTED) by pressing the **Backspace** or **Esc** key. Proceed with the /**Fi**le **S**ave operation, and 1-2-3 will save the file without the password.

To change a password, complete the first two steps for deleting the password name. After you have deleted (PASSWORD PROTECTED), press the space bar, type **p**, and press **Enter**. At this point, 1-2-3 will prompt you for a new password and ask you to verify it. Once you have completed these steps and saved the file, the new password will be stored.

1 . . . .

2 . . . .

3 . . . .

4 . . . .

Transfer

Compare how your own computer software texts and screens in English give instructions, explanations and advice with the methods used by Lotus 1-2-3.

Sales

Introduction

You are the new Sales Director of a subsidiary of a multinational company. On the way to your first international sales meeting, you check how people speak about sales in English. You do this by looking at parts of *The Manager's Handbook* published by Arthur Young International. Check that you understand the words in the list below. Task 1 shows the context in which these words are used in this unit.

Key Words

advertising agency	incentive	decision maker
advertising campaign	media	salesforce
business card	presentation	field
client	prospect	file
competitor	public relations (PR)	sponsorship
customer	salesperson	
market sector/segment	quotation	

Select a word or phrase from the Key Words list which matches one of the eight definitions given below. If you like, compare the definitions here with others in a dictionary. If there are other words in the list which you do not know, look them up too.

1 person identified as a potential buyer.
2 identifiable part of society that contains potential buyers e.g. aged between 18 and 35.
3 document or collection of data with key information.
4 a person who sells things.
5 card identifying name, position, company, etc.
6 another company which sells similar products.
7 customer for services.
8 all the people who sell for a company.

Text 1

Pre-reading

Task 2

An important task of a Sales Department is 'Prospecting'. Explain what 'Prospecting' is.

Task 3

Look at the three subtitles suggested for the extract on the next page. Any of them could be used after the word 'Prospecting'. Which is the best? Skim the text, then put them in order of preference.

a) 'A useful sales activity'
b) 'Helpful if done systematically'
c) 'An important but neglected sales activity'

Prospecting

Selling is the direct confrontation between the company and its customer. Management training and material tend to be devoted to 'closing the sale', 'effective presentation skills', 'use of visual aids', and so on. The one aspect of selling which is often neglected is 'prospecting'.

In advance of any direct selling activity or, indeed, any promotion, it is important to take time and allocate resources to prospecting for clients. Prospecting identifies buyers and makes best use of time available for selling. It is the quality, not the quantity, of prospects that matters. Market segmentation will show the market segment most likely to yield buyers, eg manufacturing companies with a turnover in excess of £5 million within 50 miles of your offices.

Building up a prime prospect file is the most valuable activity a salesperson can do. Once achieved, canvassing is necessary only to 'top up' the prospect reservoir when the level drops; that is, a prospect is converted to a customer, ceases to be a prime prospect and is replaced by another prime prospect.

The prospect file will help only if it is kept up to date and used systematically. A follow-up or bring-forward system will force you to plan your time effectively.

The selection of prospects can be done at the desk or by telephone. It involves a relatively low cost resource, compared with a field salesperson. The use of computers enables companies to develop a database of prospects which can be used interactively, depending on sales objectives or changes in strategy. By using a computerized marketing database, you can analyse important factors such as source of prospect/lead, date last called, change in staff.

A new sale in a market sector can open the door to acquiring a number of new prospects in this sector.

Task 4

On the following page is another part of the same section from *The Manager's Handbook*. It is arranged in four boxes. Look at the text but do not read it in detail.

1 Number the boxes in the correct order 1 – 4.
2 Choose a title for each box from this list:

prime prospect selection/canvassing/customer acquisition/hot prospects

a

Much time can be saved by ruthless application of the following criteria:

- Money ability to pay for your product or service, ie being able to afford it and pay for it.
- Authority: you may successfully sell to a prospect, but make sure he has the authority to buy. Don't be misled by titles on business cards. Your time may also be profitably spent finding a star who may be a real buyer in the future.
- Need: no matter how convincing your sales talk, your time is wasted if you give it to a prospect who has no need for your product.

If any of these three criteria is not met, the prospect must be discarded.

b

The final stage of the prospecting process is when a prospect is converted to a customer and a sale is made. (NB a customer may be a hot prospect for other products and services).

c

The key elements in surveying potential customers are research and creativity. The research phase identifies the names of prospects, their size, location and type of business. Sources of prospects are various and often depend on product/service. Sources of data include:

- Electoral registers
- Trade directories
- Kompass directory
- Development agency directories
- End-user lists
- Other companies' sales ledgers
- Seminars/presentations on subjects of interest
- Chamber of Commerce
- Trade Associations
- Publications

d

These are prospects who have the need to buy – now.

They must be rigorously courted and sales effort must be concentrated on the period during which they are on heat.

This is the buying time, and the opportunity must not be missed.

The following extract is also from *The Manager's Handbook*. Use the following words to help you complete the text:

a) basic b) contacts c) visits d) decision makers e) information f) database
g) data h) telephone

The Prospect File

To enable you to make well-informed judgements
and successful sales

1)   , a prospect file, or marketing

2)   , must include the following

3)   :

4)   data: company name address

5)   etc

Holding company and structure

Key personnel and 6)

Relationship with your company and

previous 7)   /jobs

Financial 8)   /performance

Recent information/activities/appointments

Text 2

Skim the left hand column of the text on the next page and decide if these sentences are true or false.

1 Selling is basically the same as any other field of management.
2 It is most effective to sell the easiest products to the easiest customers.
3 Incentive systems are usually a good idea.
4 Salespersons often don't help each other when an incentive system is in operation.
5 Chasing debts is not the responsibility of the sales force.

SELLING AND MARKETING

Selling

Management is fundamentally about direction and control. Selling is no different.

All salespeople, particularly those in large companies, present a basic problem: they enjoy spending their time doing what they know best, with the products that are easiest to sell, and selling to those customers who are easiest to sell to. Direction, management and control are needed to ensure that selling time and cost is spent where it is most effective – on prime and hot prospects.

Successful sales managers and directors keep the pressure on their sales force by meeting regularly with them to review:

- Performance versus budget
- Key performance ratios
- Follow-up procedures
- Opportunities
- Competitor activity.

Incentives do not figure high on this list. Many sales managers spend too much time inventing elaborate sales incentive schemes, which the sales-force can manipulate to their personal benefit. Incentives must be geared toward the overall objectives of the marketing plan in terms of turnover and cost. When used, they should be short, sharp and regular, enhancing the overall sales effort, not detracting from it.

Sales incentive schemes are often an excuse for poor management of the sales resource. There are many lasting benefits in creating an effective team relationship within a sales force: shared experience is a benefit that does not arise from a totally competitive environment.

The other forgotten standard of performance is control of debt. A sale is not a sale until the debt has been paid. The sales force should chase up money owed to the company. It was responsible for the sale and should be responsible for assuring its payment – before team members are paid a bonus.

How well are we doing?

The key performance indicators of selling activity are:

Ratios

- Percentage sales: budget
- Contract/orders: quotations
- (a)
- Percentage margins:sales

Salesforce

- Number of calls
- (b)
- Progress on enquiries/quotations
- Credit control (age debt of sales)
- Frequency of calls per day/week/month etc
- (c)
- Percentage discounts: sales overall utilization
- Number of customers and their value
- Administration of sales/reports/prospects
- Submission of itineraries

Overall

- Cost of sales force/sales
- (d)
- Orders to calls ratio
- Percentage discounts: sales
- (e)

Know your customer base. It may be most appropriate to spend 80 per cent of your selling/promotional activity with 20 per cent of your clients who account for 80 per cent of your turnover.

Beating the competition

Always overestimate your competitors – they are not sitting back letting you make the sale at list price and in a well-ordered process. In any competitive sale, get to know the clients better than your competitors and establish what influences their attitudes. Sales are not made to companies – they are made to individual people, whose attentions are being sought. The sales call report should be used as a source of information on competitors.

Look at the right hand column of the text on the previous page. Read it, and complete the text by putting the following phrases in the best position.

1 Length of calls
2 Quotations: leads
3 Key account development
4 Sales value/order
5 Number of new prospects called/found

One way of increasing your range of words is to learn them not individually but in 'word families'. Look at the example below and then, using your dictionary if necessary, complete the table.

	Noun(s)	Verb	Adjective
Example	manager management	to manage	managerial manageable
1	success		
2		to compete	
3	payment, payee		
4			useful
5			promotional
6		to inform	
7			manufactured
8		to value	
9		to relate	
10	analysis		

Another extract from the same section is the sales call report on the following page. Read it and decide which of the four summaries on page 29 represents it best.

The sales call report

The cornerstone of most sales control systems is the prospect client call report. The example can be modified to meet the needs of most companies and covers the essential ingredients.

If produced as part of a carbonless business form, it can greatly aid the communication process, and in particular:

- Assist managers to control sales staff.
- Establish customers' needs.
- Act as a bring-forward reminder.
- Ensure necessary action is taken by salespeople and support staff.

1 Who are you calling on?

. . . .

. . . .

. . . .

. . . .

2 Why are you calling?

. . . .

. . . .

. . . .

. . . .

. . . .

3 Result of the call.

. . . .

. . . .

. . . .

. . . .

4 Client/customer requirements etc.

. . . .

. . . .

. . . .

. . . .

5 Action required.

. . . .

. . . .

. . . .

. . . .

Arthur Young

① PROSPECT CALL REPORT — DATE 25 APR 1986 — AY CONTACT A. SMITH

PROSPECT CLIENT ULTIMATE OIL CO — CONTACT

COMPANY NAME — CONTACT NAME J. BARREL

ADDRESS ALTENS FARM ROAD ABERDEEN — POSITION MAINEN. MNG.

DECISION MAKER — IF NO WHO IS A. LOADER

TELEPHONE 0224 890000 — NAME / POSITION ADMINISTRATION MANAGER

NATURE OF BUSINESS OIL + GAS EXPLORATION — AUDIT CLIENT

WHO INITIATED CALL CLIENT/AY — IF AUDIT PARTNER N/A

PURPOSE OF VISIT

② FOLLOWING A RECENT ADVERTISEMENT WHERE ULTIMATE WERE ADVERTISING FOR INTERNAL CONSULTANTS TO ASSIST IN REORGANIZATION OF THEIR INTERNAL SYSTEMS/STRUCTURE IN THE ABERDEEN OPERATION

REPORT OF CALL

③ MET WITH MR BARREL, WHO IS NOT THE DECISION MAKER, BUT WILL PRODUCE TERMS OF REFERENCE FOR THE CONSULTANTS + WILL BE ON PRESENTATION BOARD. OUR CAPABILITY WAS PRESENTED TO HIM, AND THEIR NEEDS CONFIRMED.

PROSPECT'S INTEREST — THE CLIENT REQUIRES:

④ (A) A SECONDED CONSULTANT FOR NINE MONTHS
(B) CONSULTANT TO BE EXPERIENCED IN OIL + GAS BUSINESS, AN ENGINEER WITH SYSTEMS EXPERIENCE AND IN GENERAL MANAGEMENT/BOARD
(C) FIRM OF CONSULTANTS TO HAVE HUMAN RESOURCES AND FINANCIAL SKILLS TO COMPLEMENT SECONDED CONSULTANT

ACTION REQUIRED	BY WHOM	DATE
① SUITABLE CONSULTANTS SELECTED	AS/BOSS	5/5/86
② PROPOSAL WRITTEN AND SUBMITTED TO CLIENT	AS	19/5/86
③ PRESENTATION OF PROPOSAL	AS/BOSS	28/5/86

1 Ultimate Oil need a consultant engineer to help them improve their technical performance.
2 Ultimate Oil need a consultant, who is employed by a firm of consultants, to help them reorganise their operations in Aberdeen.
3 Ultimate Oil need another consultant to help them improve the internal systems/structure of their operation in Aberdeen.
4 Ultimate Oil need an independent consultant to advise them on new systems and structures for their Aberdeen operation.

Task 10

Read the report again and decide which of the following texts goes with each of the five headings round the sales report.

a This section records the objective of the call and establishes the criteria against which results can be measured. By completing this section, the salesperson confirms that the call will represent effective use of time.
b This section summarises the prospect's interests and justifies the action to be taken.
c This section is the basic reference which establishes if the call is being made on the decision maker, or if it is exploratory. Salespeople are often diverted to an assistant who cannot authorise a purchase.
d This section outlines the caller's proposal or presentation. The customer's response should be qualified, and any information, such as competitor activity and change in customer need, detailed.
e All sales calls require action, especially those which could result in a lost order. The salesperson will normally have to follow up the call. He/she will need to call on support services to prepare detailed quotations or dispatch products and sales literature. The most important purpose is to communicate the status of a particular customer.

Text 3

Pre-reading

Task 11

Before you read the text, use your own ideas, knowledge and experience to suggest answers to the following questions.

1 What is product promotion and what is used to promote products?
2 How does a company know if its promotions are successful or not?

Task 12

Skim the text on the next page to find out what the main techniques of promoting the business are.

Promoting the business

Even the best advertising campaigns will fail unless correct promotion has ensured a fully informed, enthusiastic and motivated public. Far from being an exact science, promotion means delivering the 'selling' message to the right public with appropriate emphasis and force.

The ingredients of promotion are: public relations, sponsorship, sales promotion and advertising – a well chosen balance of these, related to stimulating the buying urge, is the aim of a good marketing strategy. Promotion of a product, company or business is carried out by advertising or PR agencies, in-house PR or sales promotion staff. It is their accurate and sensitive marketing that makes for good promotion.

Apart from the major manufacturers of consumer goods, business in general has lost, or never developed, the art of testing. However, test marketing, or testing a promotional technique, remains a most effective way of establishing whether:

• Research results are valid
• An idea is worth developing
• Customers' reactions to change are real
• Product development expenditure is justified

Testing can therefore ensure that the considerable expenditure on sales and market promotion gives the maximum value for money.

The form of promotion depends on the 'public' to be reached. The most important of these are customers and clients – established and prospective – on whose patronage the companies' financial success depends. Increasingly, the financial community – banks, stockbrokers and shareholders – are gaining significance as a 'public'. And a vital and often overlooked group is company employees and their families; while for companies with environmental concerns, politicians are important.

Promotional activity

For any form of promotion, first set a sales goal and decide what emphasis to put on advertising, sales promotion, PR and sponsorship.

Promotional activity is used to:

- (a) greater awareness in prospective customers' minds of the company and its products.
- (b) buying easier by communicating product features/benefits.
- (c) products, services, ideas, business etc.
- (d) opinions, attitudes and hence market shares.
- (e) in order to persuade.
- (f) current customers and attract new ones.
- (g) company reputations.
- (h) number of sales calls.
- (i) priority and value of products and services.
- (j) the cost of selling yet increase its value.

Choose a suitable verb from the list below to complete the sentences (a-j) on the uses of promotional activity.

Build/Create/Change/Reduce/Inform/Sell/Upgrade/Make/Increase/Retain.

Write all the above verbs in your vocabulary notes together with (where possible) the equivalent noun form. Use a dictionary to help you if necessary.

Example: to create s.t. / creation (*n*).

Transfer

Write a report comparing the sales and promotion practices used in your company with those recommended in the texts in this unit.

Marketing

Introduction

You have been asked to prepare recommendations on how your company can improve its image, and promote its products or services. One possibility is to use an advertising agency to do this. You decide to read up on the subject, to identify advantages and disadvantages of using outside agencies, and to consider what your market research should involve. The three texts in this unit are some of the items you read during your research.

Key Words

audit	opinion	to justify
behaviour	panel	prospect(s)
corporate	to profile	to close a deal
cost-effective	to promote	survey
current	reputation	trend
experience	sample	verifiable
forecast	target	positioning
fact	growth	to boost
margin	image	to analyse

Select words or phrases from the list of Key Words on the previous page which can mean approximately the same as the phrases given below.

1 that can be checked objectively.
2 to study in detail.
3 to produce a description of a consumer, his lifestyle, habits, financial position, etc.
4 an analysis or study.
5 the place of a product in the market in terms of its capacity to meet the requirements of particular consumers.
6 consumers who are potential customers.
7 worth the money/producing increased sales.
8 to advertise/to increase consumer awareness.

Text 1

Pre-reading

The distinction between fact and opinion in a text is important. It concerns the particular views of the writer. Normally, a writer who gives opinions should offer evidence to justify them. For example:

The European Community is the largest single market in the world – comprising over 340 million consumers – 115 million more than the USA and 215 million more than Japan.

Is this fact or opinion? One possible point of dispute is the claim that Europe is a single market. Perhaps it is not a single market for certain goods and services. The writer attempts to justify his opinion by giving evidence, i.e. population figures.

Another kind of evidence to justify opinion is experience. Look at this example:

We have found that consistency is the secret to creating a clear corporate image.

We have found is approximately the same as *Our experience tells us*.

Task 2

Read the heading at the top of the following page. Do you think the article will contain fact or opinion, or both? If it contains opinions, how will the writer justify them?

Working with Advertising Agencies – The Saab-Scania Experience

by Lars Einar
Market Communications Manager,
Saab-Scania AB, Saab Car Division,
Sweden

Task 3

Now read the extract on the next page, which comes from the middle of Lars Einar's article. Remember that it is not necessary to understand every word. Identify the main points in paragraphs 3-8. The first is already done as an example.

Paragraph 3

The car business offers many ways to increase the number of prospects at dealer (showroom) level.

Paragraph 4

Paragraph 5

Paragraph 6

Paragraph 7

Paragraph 8

• Are these main points fact or opinion?

1 Market communication goes beyond mere advertising. Choosing the wrong media may be disastrous. Ask yourself this question: what is our problem – do we have too few prospects or are we not closing enough deals with the prospects we have? Let us look at the answer.

2 In 1981, we concluded that, on average, we closed a deal with one out of every five prospects who entered dealer showrooms. This meant roughly that if we sold 90,000 cars a year, 360,000 prospects out of a total of 450,000 went home without buying. By closing only two per cent more deals, we could increase our sales by 7,200 cars. So we provided sales training courses for salesmen to help them sell more efficiently, which cost SEK 4 million a year. If we had boosted advertising costs to achieve the same increase, we would have ruined our budget and our importers' budgets in no time.

3 Who has ever heard of an advertising agency suggesting sales training instead of increased advertising? If you have clearly defined target groups, you open new paths for market communication. The car business ought to offer a great many cost-effective ways of boosting the number of prospects at dealer level.

4 Unfortunately, the advertising business seems to be abandoning this approach, concentrating increasingly on adverts and TV commercials.

5 The second common mistake – from which we in particular have suffered – is that the absence of profiling and positioning targets, consistency and commitment in advertising has produced neither image nor position. Our agencies felt it was more important to come out with a new campaign every year, each one more ingenious than the previous one, but without projecting a clear-cut Saab identity.

6 According to our surveys, our target group has basically the same buying preferences in all markets. Our objective has been based on consistently spreading the same basic message about Saab in all markets and in all media.

7 But we do not want to dictate policy, as do some of our competitors. We want each one of our importers and their advertising agencies to understand and be aware of the overall Saab strategies and positioning targets, and be creative in adapting them to their own markets.

Communicating with Agencies

8 When we presented completed strategies and targets for marketing and market communication five or six years ago, our own agencies, as well as the agencies of our importers, failed to respond. It appeared that we had encroached on the agencies' territories, which they could not accept. In the past year, the general competence of advertising agencies has come under increasingly heavy criticism from various companies. Debates have raged in both the Swedish and the international press. I will just briefly run down the most critical points and those that also coincide with my own experience.

- The competence of agencies is inadequate.

Advertising agencies have specialised increasingly in straight advertising and television commercials. Many of the agencies have totally lost the ability and the interest to use the media and analyse the market. They no longer adopt an overall approach, based on knowledge of modern marketing methods, which is why less experienced advertising buyers are receiving the wrong advice, usually based on whatever is best for the agency, but not for the customer.

- The agencies are out of touch.

Many of the agencies are working the same way they did 10 to 20 years ago and have not discovered that the media developments are moving ever faster and that companies have surpassed them in marketing. What is worse, they refuse to open their eyes to the problem. They have little ability to realise the role they play, which, in complex export marketing situations, is to listen to the advertising buyers and understand their overall needs. They simply do not know how a modern corporation works.

The criterion for good advertising has been good taste.

- Having large ads incorporating unusual concepts is more important than the practical aspect.

They prize creative freedom and ignore all talk of targets, strategies, profits and budget.

- Agencies find it difficult to work together, even when they are working for the same client. They fight with competing agencies who have specialised in printed matter, direct mail advertising, sales training and so on, and regard these activities as worthless.

- Aency rates and media costs have reached the limit of what many companies are prepared to pay.

Read the section headed *Communicating with Agencies* again.

1 What is the writer's opinion of advertising agencies?
2 What evidence does he provide to justify his opinions?

Text 2

Pre-reading

Here are some possible advantages in using an advertising agency.
Discuss whether they are *genuine* advantages, then list them in order of importance.

1 knowledge of the domestic and international market
2 experts in design
3 knowledge of the media (newspapers, magazines, radio and television)
4 good printing techniques
5 easier to use an agency than to co-ordinate everything yourself
6 independent and objective opinion
7 cheaper than using various suppliers, or employing own staff

Task 5

Skim the extract from the essay *Advertising* by John Hobson in *The Gower Handbook of Management*. Do not read the text in detail. Only decide if the writer is giving fact or opinion.

THE AGENCY RELATIONSHIP

The basic contribution of the agency must be its expertise in particular services – top creative ability, experienced media men for selecting and buying media, good technicians in the printing and
5 blockmaking and other mechanical processes, and competent co-ordination, at executive level, of all the many details of a campaign. It is possible for an advertiser to buy many of these services from specialists outside the service agency, but, in the UK
10 at least, there is no real sign that advertisers prefer to take on the job of co-ordinating such outside services themselves. The agency package is still the most convenient method.
There is, however, one other great value in the
15 agency arrangement. The manufacturer tends to look at his marketing proposition from the boardroom downwards. He relates it to his manufacturing, profits, raw materials, distribution and the like. It is,
to many manufacturers, an enormous advantage to
20 have the compensating service of people who look at the same proposition from the market upwards. This is the special competence of the good agency. The manufacturer's personnel, even if they have the ability and training to take a consumer's view may, in
25 certain circumstances, not have the independence to prevail on the board to make essential changes. The agency is an independent body and will be listened to more readily by the board. Finally the manufacturer, being concerned with his own type of business and
30 immersed in it, may not have had the useful experience of outside industries, of successes and failures in other related or unrelated fields, which an agency with many clients can gather together. The manufacturer values someone competent to trade
35 ideas with as a means of measuring his own interests against outside criticism.

---

1 Scan the text and note all the advantages of using an advertising agency that Hobson mentions.
2 Compare Hobson's views with the ideas in Text 1. Are they the same?

Task 7

Notice in the extract on the previous page how each sentence has a topic or subject at or near the beginning of the sentence, and ends with the comment or what is said *about* the topic. Here are two examples from the first paragraph.

LINE	TOPIC	COMMENT
1	The basic contribution of the advertising agency	expertise in particular services
8	an advertiser	(can buy) services from specialists outside the agency

Complete the following by identifying either the topic or the comment.

LINE	TOPIC	COMMENT
12	agency package	a ....
15	b	looks at marketing proposition from above downwards
23	the manufacturer's personnel	c ....
28	the manufacturer	d ....

Task 8

Long sentences are often difficult to understand. One way to help clarify the meaning is to understand the relationships between words which refer to the same thing. Writers use different words to avoid repetition, for example:

A marketing strategy dominated by low pricing is a risky policy for small companies in competitive markets; *it* can easily be countered by larger concerns *who* can afford a temporary drop in prices, while* *they* also offer greater security to the customer.

What do the words in *italics* in the above text refer to?

NOTE
* The word *while* is often used in this way, meaning *and at the same time*.

Here is a section of the text on *The Agency Relationship* from page 36 rewritten with a lot of repetition. Underline the repeated parts, and decide which word or words were used in the original to avoid the repetition. Then look again at the text to check your answers.

There is, however, one other great value in the agency arrangement. The manufacturer tends to look at the manufacturer's marketing proposition from the boardroom downwards. The manufacturer relates the manufacturer's marketing proposition to the manufacturer's
5 manufacturing, profits, raw materials, distribution and the like. It is to many manufacturers an enormous advantage to have the compensating service of people who look at the same proposition from the market upwards. Looking at the same proposition from the market upwards is the special competence of the good agency. The manufacturer's personnel,
10 even if the manufacturer's personnel have the ability and training to take a customer's view may, in certain circumstances, not have the independence to prevail upon the board to make essential changes.

Text 3

Pre-reading

The text below, from an Arthur Young International management training publication, is about market research. The writer claims that this is essential when you are preparing a market plan. Before you read the text, what do you think needs to be considered in market research?

Look only at the headings in the text below and see if the writer has included the same things that you have thought about above. What does the writer think are the essential elements in market research?

Market research

Marketing plans and changes in direction should be based on verifiable data.
Analyse the last five years'
5 performance and use forecasts and published indices to predict the behaviour of customers and markets in the future. Forecast at 'current prices'. Remember that every
10 forecast you make will be wrong. Sound research-based judgement will help you to be sufficiently accurate to make key strategic decisions.
15 A review of performance can take one of the following forms.

1 External audit

The market: total market, size, growth and trends (value/volume). Market character: developments and trends, products, distribution
5 channels, customers/consumers, communication, industry practices. Competition: size, share, standing and reputation; marketing methods, production capabilities,
10 diversification, profitability, key strengths and weaknesses.

2 Internal audit

Sales: by location, type, customer, product.

Market shares: profit margins, cost rates.
5 Marketing mix variables: product management, price, distribution, promotion, operations and resources.

3 Customer research

Customer requirements and habits: some organisations use panels of sample consumers to gauge the acceptability of the product or
5 change in product/price. In industrial marketing, research is often ignored, and questions are seldom asked of buyers as to their satisfaction and future needs.

Earlier in this unit the difference between fact and opinion was examined. This text contains suggestions. Identify four suggestions and decide if you agree with them or not.

Provide alternative words or expressions for the following words that appear in the text.

1   verifiable (line 3)
2   behaviour (7)
3   forecast (8)
4   forecast (10)
5   sound (11)
6   growth (External audit – 2)
7   standing (External audit – 7)
8   requirements (Customer research – 1)
9   panels of sample consumers (Customer research – 2/3)
10 to gauge (Customer research – 3)
11 seldom (Customer research – 8)

Transfer

Use information from the texts in this unit – and also your own knowledge, opinions and experience – to write a memo to your Managing Director suggesting ways to improve your company's image and its sales. Include suggestions for market research and possible use of an advertising agency – depending on your point of view.

Computer Systems

Introduction

Your department is planning to buy new computer equipment. You must prepare a report which includes information on the advantages of integration between computers, ways to reduce costs, and the alternatives available in expanding computing capability.

This unit contains three texts with relevant information for your report. Check that you understand all the words below. If you have problems, try Task 1 first, then look up the words in a dictionary.

Key Words

access	linking	equipment
advantage	to monitor	incompatibility
benefit	network	workstation
clone	to proliferate	standardisation
consultant	printer	
to plug together	drawback	

Explain the words in italics in the sentences below. Give alternative words in English.

1 *Incompatibility* between different pieces of *equipment* makes *linking* impossible.
2 A major *advantage* of using *clones* is they are usually cheaper than the original versions.
3 *Standardisation* of equipment has obvious *benefits*.
4 Independent *consultants* can advise on what equipment to buy when you plan to develop a *network* of terminals.
5 One *drawback* of having a *printer* at every *workstation* is the high cost.
6 Under-used computer equipment can *proliferate* in large companies without a system to *monitor* purchasing.

Text 1

Pre-reading

Task 2

Before you read the text, using your knowledge or experience, answer the following questions.

1 What are the advantages of integration?
2 Why is integration often difficult?
3 What are the important factors if you want to connect two computers?
4 Look only at the title, diagram and introduction below. What do you think the article is about? What does the picture represent?

CHAPTER 5
INTEGRATION • LOCAL AREA NETWORKS

**LINKING EQUIPMENT –
THE FULLY AUTOMATED BUSINESS**

Sooner or later every business will begin to consider the benefits of integration. Linking computer systems together makes clear economic sense even in small companies. But how can the forward looking business prepare for integration? And what options exist for the larger company that may wish to link all its electronic equipment into a single 'local area network'?

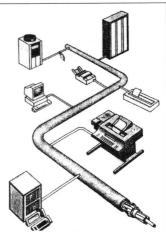

The first sentence of a paragraph often tells us what the paragraph is about. For this reason, the first sentence is very important in understanding. When skimming a text, pay more attention to the beginning of a paragraph than to the middle or end.

To illustrate this, look at the sentences below. These are the first sentences from the five paragraphs in the article on the following page. They are in the correct order. Reading these sentences should give you a good idea of what the text is about.

1 For most users the first kind of integration of equipment that will be required is between two single-user microcomputers.

2 Once this happens it soon becomes obvious that linking the machines together provides clear benefits.

3 The linking of equipment in this way can provide other benefits too.

4 Unfortunately, for the small company that has invested in a number of single-user microcomputers, integration is not simply a matter of plugging equipment together.

5 Indeed, linking equipment in this way is so complex that it is essential for any growing business to think about the problem before purchasing.

• Write down, in a few words, what you think each paragraph is probably about.

The five paragraphs appear on the next page without the opening sentences above. They are in the wrong order. Match the sentences above to the appropriate paragraph. The first is done for you, as an example.

a) *Once this happens it soon becomes obvious that linking the machines together provides clear benefits.* Users can work on the same centralised data so that, for example, a credit controller can know exactly what state a customer's account is in at any time. Centralising the data like this means that duplication of work effort is minimised too. For example a sales department need not enter details of a new customer if the details have already been entered in a centralised data store by another operator.

b) .... A range of factors must be considered. Is the processing speed of the two machines the same? Are the screen displays the same size? Will data in a disk respond to commands input at a workstation elsewhere in the office, working on different software?

c) .... If the company is aiming at integration sometime in the future, it should buy suitable equipment from the start. This means either investing in hardware that is designed to link together through a central controller, or in single-user microcomputers that can run software which enables the machines to exchange information and understand each other.

d) .... The most common of these is internal electronic mail. Messages can easily be sent from one operator to another as long as they share the same data store. And, for example, in a business where a great deal of word processing is carried out, standard letters and documents can be stored centrally so that any of the users attached to the system can gain access to them. Multi-user systems therefore, for any but the smallest company, make clear sense.

e) .... Many small companies buy a single microcomputer and then, as workloads increase or as the microcomputer proves itself more and more important in the business, additional machines are purchased.

Give one or more alternatives for the following words which appear in the text on the previous page.

benefits (para. a, line 2)		processing speed	(b, 2)
input	(b, 4)	aiming	(c, 2)
enables	(c, 5)	share	(d, 3)
carried out	(d, 5)	access	(d, 7)
workloads	(e, 2)	purchased	(e, 4)

Task 5

Scan the same text for information to complete the following table.

1) Advantages of computer interconnection:
2) Factors affecting integration:

Text 2

Pre-reading

Task 6

The illustration on the next page is an extract from the magazine *Which Computer?* Look at the title and the illustration. What do you think the article which follows it in the magazine is about? Does it talk about hardware or software?

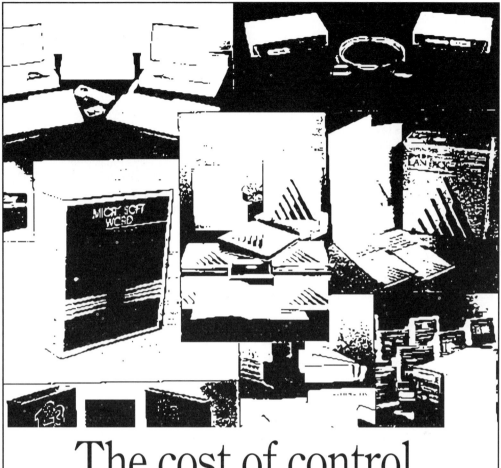

The cost of control

Task 7

This exercise looks at headings. Here are the six section headings for the article on the following page. They are in the correct order. Consider each of the headings. What do you think they mean?

1 Monitoring and controlling printer output
2 Memory use
3 Outside consultants
4 Standardisation and rigorous justification
5 Orderly disposal
6 Software: weighing the alternatives

The six sections of the article appear in the wrong order. Match each section with the right heading above. Do not read the text in detail yet – only skim it. Do not stop to think about words you do not know.

a. When machines become outdated there is a tendency to move them into other departments that have not previously been computerised. Are the recipients really going to benefit, or is the object of the exercise primarily to clear the desks of the initial users to make way for the new machines? The same rigorous criteria have to be applied to the reinstallation of used machines as for the assessment of new purchases. If the department about to get lumbered with an old machine really does need to go computerised shouldn't you consider supplying it with new equipment? A really out of date machine may literally be more trouble than it is worth. You might be better to consider selling it cheaply for the personal use of your staff at home or giving it to a local school or charity.

b. Do you know the destination and purpose of every copy of every document generated? Properly vetted mailing lists might reduce your printer requirements by 15 per cent. Email may be a more efficient substitute for inter-departmental and inter-branch memos. Are departments producing too many internal documents as a result of unsatisfactory display equipment or poor organisation? Perhaps much of the data need never appear in print at all.

c. If you are buying 200 copies of a spreadsheet for use throughout the company, and may buy 200 more next year, the difference between £300 per package for the industry standard and £99 per package for a reliable clone that may have additional useful features is a tidy £80,000. Are your software evaluators playing safe at the company's expense? Or is there a case to be made for paying the extra for support and security? Somebody should at least be arguing the case.

d. PCs have proliferated in the past three years, and when it comes to assessing their individual utility to the company the insider often finds it hard to see the wood for the trees. Issues like departmental rivalry, emotional involvement and job status make it worthwhile considering calling in a firm of outside consultants to find out which PCs are really working for you and which are simply soaking up desk space and would be better employed elsewhere.

e. Fast memory is expensive, tape-based backing store is slow but cheap. Between these two is a range of disk storage where speed is traded off against cost. Is your mainframe system optimised to keep data in the appropriate place, with the least frequently accessed data stored on the slow media and the more often reviewed files in core? Or is poor organisation forcing you to buy more fast memory than you need?

f. In the past many companies have allowed PC purchases to be made out of a variety of departmental budgets with no central control. This results in mixed standards and uncertainty about future connectivity as well as software incompatibility and support problems. The spend is almost as hard to quantify as the benefits. Most well organised companies have now replaced this free-for-all with a centralised purchasing authority that short-lists approved manufacturers and requires rigorous justification for each machine purchased. Six-monthly or annual reviews of machine use against the same criteria may very possibly free machines for re-allocation, reducing the number of future purchases required.

Below are six potential problems with computer hardware and software cost control.

1 incompatibility between different machines and software
2 the company prints too much – uses a lot of paper!
3 internal disagreement on what to buy
4 very high software costs
5 unused out of date equipment
6 very high cost of memory hardware

Decide if any of these match your own company's experience. Select three problems. Find suggested solutions in the text on the previous page and take notes. What do you think of the suggestions?

Task 9

The following words occur in the text on the previous page. Find the words and use the context to give the probable meaning. Even if you are not sure, have a guess.

assessing (para. d)   clone (c)
outdated (a)   allowed (f)
spreadsheet (f)   Email (b)
vetted (b)   recipients (a)

To revise the eight words above, complete the memo below, which is from the Financial Director of a large company to her secretary. Put one word in each space.

JMS COMMUNICATIONS LTD

Memorandum

From: J. Coltrane

To: Ruth A. S.

Pls send the following message by a) .... to all departments:
Any expenditure to replace b) ....equipment or to
buy c) .... software must be closely d) ....
e) .... all alternatives takes time but is worthwhile. A cheaper
f) .... may be better value.
Eventual g) .... of new equipment must report use of
equipment during the first six months.
Purchases are not h) .... without the approval of the
department Managing Director.

Text 3

Pre-reading

Imagine a situation where a company has a computer, or perhaps several computers, but anyone who wants to use one must wait. The company therefore needs more computers. The text below discusses an aspect of this problem – interconnection. Before reading the text, consider the following questions.

1 What other word, already used in this unit, is similar to 'interconnection'?
2 What alternatives are available for the company in the above situation?

Skim the text – do not read it in detail yet – and identify three alternatives to the standalone computer.

Sooner or later you'll need to give more than one person access to the computer. There will come a time when two urgent tasks clash and you'll be forced to make a crucial decision you should have made months earlier.

One easy solution is to buy another standalone computer when you need it and link the two together with special software and a hard disk. This will be expensive. An alternative is a multi-user machine to which you simply add extra terminals as and when you need them; this can work out cheaper.

There is a drawback though. Multi-user micro suppliers usually claim their machines support up to, say, 16 users but 10 is more realistic. When such a system is overloaded, you might find yourself typing in information faster than the computer can accept it.

But today's supermicro now has the speed and power of a minicomputer. In fact, a supermicro can quite often out-perform a mini at a fraction of the price. However, there is a realistic limit to the number of users who can share a multi-user micro. On the other hand, most minis have an upgrade path with resources to accomodate more than 100 users.

Although there have been changes due to industry standard operating systems like Unix, minicomputer suppliers have a tendency to use their own operating systems and applications software written in their own languages. This limits your choice of software and leaves you vulnerable to changes in marketing policy.

This is where multi-user micros pick up a few points. They run industry standard software so you have access to a large number of applications from a wide range of sources. If you become dissatisfied with a machine, or a supplier, you can change without scrapping all your software and starting from the beginning.

In general, only pick a multi-user micro if your staff have a limited need to use the computer, or if your departments are unlikely to expand beyond the capability of the computer to support them.

If they do, consider a network. Theoretically, there's no limit to the number of users, or to the number who can share information or other resources like printers.

Networks differ from minis and micros in one significant way. Each user can have his or her own computer instead of having to share what would otherwise be an overworked and overcrowded single processor. Networks link micros to other micros, micros to minis and minis to mainframes: in fact, any computer to any other, or to any peripheral device.

More importantly, with a network each department has its own computer without being cut off from other departments or information held elsewhere. For example, the accounts department can easily look at information held by the stock distribution department. Networks also cut down waiting time and facilitate contact with people who are often outside the office.

However, managing a network is not always a bed of roses. Of all the problems with computers, those associated with networks can be the most difficult to solve. The source of a breakdown can be nowhere near the breakdown itself. Anything from the poor siting of connection cables to system software faults can be the cause of major headaches, so it helps to know what is connected to what and where each cable goes.

Task 12

Identify some advantages and disadvantages of each alternative then complete the chart below:

Alternative	Advantages	Disadvantages
1	easy solution	2 . . . .
multi-user microcomputer/ supermicro	speed and power of minicomputer 3 . . . . 4	5 . . . .
minicomputer	speed and power 6	7 . . . . and . . . .
8	9 . . . . 10 . . . . 11	12 . . . .

Note
There are several advantages to choose from for questions 9, 10 and 11.

Transfer

Use the information in this unit, but also your own experience, to prepare either a short presentation, or a short written report. In the report you should describe the benefits of computer integration, ways to keep costs down, and the alternatives available when planning to increase computing capability.

Human Resources

Introduction

You are the Human Resources Manager of a Southeast Asian manufacturing company. Your company wants to set up a factory inside the European Community. This will be the first factory outside your home country. The Managing Director has asked you to research the costs of placing senior managers in a European country, and to investigate what other problems there might be.

Check that you understand the following words, using a dictionary if necessary. Task 1 looks at common collocations involving eight of the words in the list.

Key Words

appointment	paycheck	factory
assignment	recruitment	turnover
employee	salary	venture
to earn	survey	expenses
to compare	survival	
to negotiate	tax	

Use an appropriate form of a word from the list on the previous page to create acceptable collocations using the prompts given below. The first is done for you as an example.

1 ...... *Salary*.. negotiations   5 to conduct ....

2 annual ....   6 to pay ....

3 .... a living   7 to fix ....

4 to claim ....   8 a joint ....

Text 1

Task 2

Skim the following extract from a book called *Going International*.
What title would you give to the story?

a How to do business in Saudi Arabia
b Too many cups of coffee
c Learning the hard way

When the Saudi government announced that it was going to invest several million dollars in communications technology, an American businessman went to Riyadh to 'get something going'. His plane fare and expenses for a week were projected to be $3700. He arrived on a Monday, checked into his hotel and began making phone calls to the 'obvious points of contact'. To his surprise he could not track down anyone to see regarding his business. By Wednesday he discovered that most offices were closed on Thursday afternoon and on Friday, the Islamic day of prayer. There was nothing he could do but extend his stay and hope for better luck next week.

Eventually he made several appointments, but in each case he was frustrated by hour-or-more waits, interrupted meetings, endless cups of coffee, and instructions to 'come back another day'. He was particularly unsettled by the Arab habit of straying from the subject. After a month he ran into an old army buddy who introduced him to the basic rules of Saudi etiquette and how to do business with the Arabs. He was horrified to discover that he had repeatedly insulted his contacts by his thinly disguised impatience, refusal to take coffee, rush to talk business, aggressive selling, occasional swearing, exposing the sole of his shoe when sitting on the floor, and even when he conversationally asked an Arab official about his wife. By now his trip had cost well over $13,000 and he had only established himself as an arrogant, rude and untrustworthy American. He learned too late the three secrets to successful business in Saudi Arabia: patience, relationship building, and respect for the Arab and his ways.

Text 2

The next text, from the magazine *International Management*, also gives examples of problems in international business. Scan it to find the information to complete the table which is on the following page.

THE PRACTICE OF MANAGEMENT

BUILDING BRIDGES OVER THE CULTURAL RIVERS

A growing number of multinationals are training their staff to work in other, particularly oriental, cultures, hoping to avoid the waste from non-communication

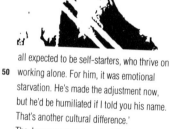

An Asian engineer is assigned to a U.S. laboratory and almost suffers a nervous breakdown. A U.S. executive tells his staff he's going to treat them fairly – and creates
5 dissension. A Japanese manager is promoted by his British president, but within six months asks for a transfer.

Each of these real-life cases involved people who were regarded as superior employees,
10 but were ill-equipped to cope with the complexities and dangers of intercultural management.

'Multinational companies have studied everything else; now they're finally looking at
15 culture,' says Clifford Clarke, founder and president of the California-based IRI International Inc., one of a small but growing number of consulting firms that specialise in teaching business people from differing
20 cultures how to communicate and work with each other.

'Never show the sole of your shoe to an Arab; never arrive on time for a party in Brazil; and in Japan, don't think 'yes' means 'yes','

25 advise U.S. consultants Lennie Copland and Lewis Brown Griggs, who have produced a series of films and a book to help managers improve their international business skills. But simply learning the social 'dos' and
30 'don'ts' is not the answer, according to the new culture specialists. The penalties for ignoring different thinking patterns, they point out, can be disastrous.

For example, the American manager who
35 promised to be fair thought he was telling his Japanese staff that their hard work would be rewarded; but when some workers received higher salary increases than others, there were complaints. 'You told us you'd be fair,
40 and you lied to us,' accused one salesman. 'It took me a year and a half,' sighed the American, 'to realise that 'fair', to my staff, meant being treated equally.'

The Asian engineer who suffered in America
45 was the victim of another mistaken expectation. 'He was accustomed to the warm group environment so typical in Japan,' said his U.S. manager. 'But in our company, we're

all expected to be self-starters, who thrive on
50 working alone. For him, it was emotional starvation. He's made the adjustment now, but he'd be humiliated if I told you his name. That's another cultural difference.'

The Japanese manager who failed to respond
55 to his promotion couldn't bring himself to use the more direct language needed to communicate with his London-based superiors. 'I used to think all this talk about cultural communication was a lot of baloney,'
60 says Eugene J. Flath, president of Intel Japan Ltd., a subsidiary of the American semiconductor maker. 'Now, I can see it's a real problem.' Miscommunication has slowed our ability to coordinate action with
65 our home office.'

That's why Intel, with the help of consultant Clarke, began an intercultural training programme this spring which Flath expects will dramatically reduce decision-making
70 time now lost in making sure the Americans and the Japanese understand each other.

© Copyright International

Number	Person	Cause of problem	Result of problem
Example	American businessman in Saudi Arabia	He didn't know the 'rules'	He spent too much and didn't do any business
1	American manager with Japanese staff		
2	Asian engineer in the U.S.A.		
3	Japanese manager in the U.K.		

Prefixes

One way of increasing the number of words you know is to learn the meanings of the most common prefixes – elements joined to the beginnings of words to add to or change the meaning.

Example: **multi** = many   **Multinational** companies are companies that operate in many countries.

The following prefixes are all used in the text on page 52. List the words in which they are used. Their meanings are given in brackets to help you.

pro-	(forward)	inter-	(between)
trans-	(across)	super-	(above)
semi-	(half)	sub-	(under)
co-	(with)		

Note

Line 10 contains the word *ill-equipped*, where *ill-* is an adverb. What do you think it means? Other similar collocations using the adverb *ill-* are *ill-prepared*, *ill-judged*, and *ill-advised*.

Task 5

What do these words mean?

transatlantic	supersonic
interconnection	co-operate
semi-circular	propel
submarine	

Task 6

Now look at this table of the other most common prefixes and their meanings. Think of an example for each one.

Prefix	Meaning	Prefix	Meaning
ab-	away from	anti-	against
bi-	double	contra-	against
de-	reduce, reverse	ex-	out of
il- ir- im- in-	not	micro-	small
mis-	bad, wrong	post-	after
pre-	before	re-	do again

• Create a file containing groups words, each group with a different prefix.

Text 3

Pre-reading

Task 7

When your company has a subsidiary in a foreign country, you must decide how much to pay company managers who work there. The pay they get will be related to the pay levels that are normal in the country. Look at the table below. Find the difference between the three different types of pay – gross, net and adjusted.

PAY AND PURCHASING POWER COMPARISONS FOR MANAGING DIRECTORS

COUNTRY	GROSS PAY £000s	NET PAY £000s	ADJUSTED PAY £000s	RANKING
USA (New York)	100.53	64.28	70.95	1
Switzerland	85.27	57.20	46.35	2
France	67.36	47.56	45.89	3
Italy	82.83	44.65	43.82	4
Germany	73.16	43.93	42.12	5
Japan	95.19	57.78	36.92	6
Austria	67.05	37.92	35.31	7
Australia	51.97	29.46	35.16	8
Spain	57.82	33.35	34.52	9
United Kingdom	49.87	33.54	33.54	10
Netherlands	72.08	32.00	31.75	11
South Africa	32.20	19.87	28.02	12
Belgium	63.33	27.80	27.31	13
Finland	75.00	31.78	25.71	14
Norway	55.86	31.43	24.44	15
Ireland	47.28	24.16	23.46	16
Denmark	69.18	24.29	20.64	17
Sweden	57.80	21.55	18.45	18
Portugal	23.17	13.90	17.44	19
Greece	23.75	13.35	15.02	20

© Copyright International Management

55

When you look at how much you will need to pay the managing director and other senior managers of a subsidiary located in Europe, which is the best country for you? Rank Spain, the United Kingdom, Belgium and Finland in order of preference.

Task 9

In texts on statistical subjects, you can often get nearly all the most important information simply by looking at the numbers, diagrams and tables etc. Skim the text below and find any useful information which is not in the table above.

Text 4

Task 10

In the book *Managing Cultural Differences*, there is a section about the timing of cultural awareness training. Here are five paragraphs. Their first sentences are given below in the correct order. Below them are the paragraphs. Read the first sentences to get the general idea of the text. Then decide which sentence goes with which paragraph.

1 Various opinions exist on when it is most appropriate to provide cultural awareness input, and how long it should take.

2 The real issue, however, involves organisational representatives assigned outside their native culture for short- or long-term visits.

3 The length of time devoted to preparation for foreign deployment varies according to the organisation and the availability of time and finances for training.

4 Program planners in the Canadian International Development Agency believe timing is a critical factor.

5 The 'when' of training also depends on the different information needs of participants in the training.

a .... Some non-profit agencies devote a year prior to departure for such preparation, beginning with self-study and weekly meetings, and gradually accelerating the amount of time devoted to cross-cultural and related training in group settings. One major multinational corporation devotes three to six months to getting the employee and the family ready for assignments abroad.

b   .... Many trainers maintain that such educational programs belong in professional schools and continuing education classes.

c   .... When engaged in international relations work, service or business, cross-cultural knowledge and skills are integral to the role requirements. Some believe cultural training should be given before going abroad, while others opt for such training only after arrival in the host culture. Still others insist that it must be a combination of before, during and after the overseas assignment.

d   .... There is an interaction between 'survival' information needs (schools, doctors, housing, compensation, etc.) and other information needs (adjusting to the new society, how to get the job done, making new friends, effective functioning in society, etc.). The interaction is illustrated in Figure 1.

e   .... If too close to departure, trainee anxiety may block learning. Without foreign experience, the volunteers find it hard to focus on the input. Therefore CIDA prefers to emphasise recruitment and selection for the overseas tour, and concentrate on in-country training. Whether circumstances or opinions dictate a long- or short-term approach to cross-cultural training, it is the quality of that training that is most important.

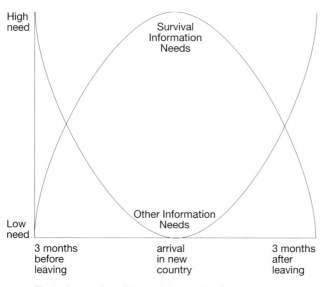

Fig 1. Interaction of the various needs of cross-cultural trainees

Transfer 1

Use information from the texts you have read to advise your Managing Director on the need for intercultural training and on the salaries paid to Managing Directors inside the EC. Do Task 11 before you begin your report.

Task 11

Which of the following sentences are correct and could be used in your report?

1 We should not expect quick results in international business.
2 Multinational companies have studied intercultural problems for many years.
3 Being 'fair' is different in different cultures.
4 Sweden's taxes are among the lowest in Europe.
5 Cross-cultural training should always be done before leaving the home country.
6 Information about housing is a 'survival' need.

Transfer 2

Write a short report for your Managing Director giving details of your ideas on the strategies and plans the company should have for sending senior managers to work abroad.

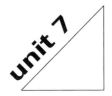

Business Travel

Introduction

You are responsible for all travel by company employees. You are worried about the way the travel budget has increased and about the effect of too much travel on some employees. You are preparing a memo on these subjects for middle and senior management. Check that you understand the Key Words. Try Task 1 before you use your dictionary.

Key Words

liberalisation	itinerary	to update
compulsory	merger	independent
deal	monopoly	stopover
destination	restriction	high-yield
discount	schedule	

Fill the gaps in the paragraph below by adding the correct form of an appropriate word from the list of Key Words.

The 1) . . . . of air transport should result in more choice of 2) . . . . and better 3) . . . . for the consumer. The large state airlines operating the majority of flights to certain destinations have a near 4) . . . . but increased competition from 5) . . . . companies will improve travellers' 6) . . . . and increase the number of flights offered at a 7) . . . . Some airports make daytime flying 8) .to avoid disturbance at night. This kind of 9) . . . . .could affect your 10). . . . . Many long-haul flights have 11). . . . . en route. In contrast to the benefits of liberalisation, consumers are often worried by any 12). . . . . between two airlines, as this can reduce choice and even create new monopolies.

Text 1

Note
Prices may be very different now to those given in Texts 1 and 2. The articles are included here as the principle of cost comparison is timeless.

Some airlines offer special deals for business travellers but there are often restrictions. Scan the *Executive Travel* article about Wardair flights on the following page, then put **S** in the box if you get the same service on the premium Apex flights as on regular business class flights or **D** (different) if you don't.

1 Destinations	5 Quality
2 Price	6 Minimum stay
3 Advance booking	7 Cabin zone
4 Comfort	8 Seating

HALF PRICE BUSINESS CLASS

WARDAIR's premium class Apex fare lets you fly to Canada in business class comfort for almost half the normal cost. Unlike British Airways and Air Canada, Wardair markets an executive excursion to all its Canadian destinations, but you must book at least 21 days ahead and stay away a minimum of seven days. There's no sacrifice in comfort or quality as the 30-seat executive zone on Wardair's Airbus A310 features roomy pitch. There's a 2 x 2 x 2 configuration (a layout some airlines use in first class) and ample 46in. legroom.

Examples of the cheaper fares are shown below.

Contact: 0800-234444

Destinations	Wardair premium Apex return	Wardair regular (unrestricted) business class return
Montreal	£750	£1,120
Ottawa	£750	£1,212
Toronto	£750	£1,246
Winnipeg	£750	£1,344
Calgary/Edmonton	£775	£1,426
Vancouver	£800	£1,428

When you are reading, it is often possible to guess the meaning of a new word by looking at its context – at what comes before it and after it. For example, the words *premium class* in the first line of the text above must mean 'special quality' because we read that you get the best comfort at a lower than normal price. Try to get the meaning of the following words by looking at them in context.

1 fare   a) travel ticket b) ticket price c) journey
2 book   a) reserve b) brochure c) read
3 sacrifice   a) extra b) loss c) equality
4 configuration   a) size b) calculation c) arrangement
5 ample   a) less than enough b) enough c) more than enough

Text 2

Skim the text on the following page from an article in *International Management* and say what the author's main message is. Then scan the article and answer the following questions.

1) Compare costs on the London–Paris, London–New York and London–Athens routes.
2) Find the problems with discount tickets.
3) Find the best airline to fly on the following routes:
   a) London – Amsterdam
   b) Dublin – Brussels
   c) London – Maastricht

HOW TO BEAT EUROPE'S SKY-HIGH AIR FARES

There is good news for business fliers who are fed up with having to pay outrageous prices for tickets. Independent airlines are challenging the monopolies of the state-dominated carriers on some key routes in Europe, offering low fares and fewer booking restrictions. And the European Commission's liberalisation package that became effective January 1 paves the way for cheaper economy as well as discount fares. Nevertheless, complications still plague the structure of European air fares. Calculated in cost per mile, the 50-minute trip from London to Paris is five times more expensive than the eight-hour trip from London to New York. London–Athens costs $20 more than London–New York, a trip of more than twice the distance. Both these are for 'unrestricted' tickets. Of course you can fly on a discount ticket which can be as low as 30% of normal economy. But these are so hedged about with restrictions, such as a compulsory Saturday night stay, advance booking or limits on flights, as to frustrate their use for business travel, where you need to be able to cancel or change a flight at the last minute.

Business travellers, who represent about 40% of total air traffic and perhaps 70% of revenue, are the geese who lay the golden eggs. I don't know of any other industry that forces customers using its products or services most to pay the highest premiums. The term 'high-yield' passenger says it all. The solution airlines have found is to segregate the 'high-yield' fliers from discount travellers by placing a movable curtain in an economy cabin with similar seats and configuration and calling it 'business class'. But there are still no price breaks for the business flier.

Enter the independent airlines. One of the first to offer a cheap flexible fare was British Midland, who provided a one-class business service on the highly competitive London–Amsterdam route. The full economy round-trip is $273 (same as British Airways or KLM whose business class is $324). Then there is a three-day return for $214 (you pay the full fare if you stay longer) as well as the usual cheap discount fares.

If you plan to travel between Dublin and Brussels (via London), you can combine economy and flexibility by flying Ryanair, an independent Irish airline that offers one-class service with unrestricted fares at less than half the price of Aer Lingus, BA and Sabena. Since Ryanair came on the scene two years ago, traffic between Dublin and London has increased by 54%.

Virgin Atlantic, which in my opinion provides the best business class value on the North Atlantic (London Gatwick to Newark), offers a one-way unrestricted fare of $63 (plus an $18 weekend surcharge) between Gatwick and Maastricht, a small town in southeast Holland – a business route all its own, with convenient road and rail access to Cologne, Dusseldorf and Eindhoven.

© Copyright International Management

Synonyms
Find words in the text on the previous page with the same meanings as these words or phrases. The words in the text occur in the same order as words 1-8.

1 extremely important
2 deregulation
3 reduced
4 journey

5 income
6 separate
7 return
8 extra charge

Text 3

Task 6

The central part of many business texts is the statistical information they contain. One good way of getting an idea of what these texts are about is to skim the numbers. Skim the following text by finding out what these numbers refer to:

48, 250–280, 280, 80–90, 60–70, 120, 300,000, 27, 150–200

New York, Los Angeles, San Diego, Phoenix, Houston, Dallas, Pittsburgh, Chicago, Minneapolis, Boston, New York, Miami, Atlanta, Tulsa, Atlanta, New York, San Francisco, Hartford, Newark, Washington, Philadelphia, New York, Cologne, London, Milan, Paris, London, Milan, London, Milan, Rome, Madrid, Milan, Tulsa, Washington, Milan, Tokyo, Milan, Atlanta, London, Milan, Amsterdam, Milan, Hannover, Paris, Milan, Amsterdam, Milan

Just reciting this list would make most of us tired. Actually visiting all these cities would comprise a busy travel year for many international executives. But for Giorgio Ronchi, these 48 destinations represent a mere three months of business travel. He expects to notch up 250 to 280 days of travel this year, a rate he has maintained for 18 months and expects to keep up for at least another year.

If you're considering hitting Ronchi's target of 280 days, you would have to travel constantly from January 1 to October 6, without a break, even on weekends. If you managed that, you could take the rest of the year off to catch up on paperwork or recover from open-heart surgery.

Even Ronchi seems amazed at his travel schedule. He points out that he spends 80–90 hours in the air each month, well above the 60–70 hours clocked by airline pilots and crews. 'I've been approaching the world record,' he declares, a broad smile beaming from his healthy, rested face.

Less hectic travellers can probably learn something from such 'record' holders. The first lesson is probably to be sure that so much travel is really necessary. Many experts claim it can be fatal. Cary L. Cooper, a management psychologist at the University of Manchester in Britain and author of *Living with Stress*, says that about 120 days of travel a year, or less than half of Ronchi's total, is the absolute limit for those who want to stay healthy and sane. When Ronchi's schedule was described to him, he replied: 'You're kidding. This is a joke – isn't it?'

Aside from the punishment it inflicts on one's body, mental health and family, it's also very expensive. Ronchi's travel expenses this year are expected to hit GB £170,000 ($300,000).

But despite the financial and personal costs, Ronchi insists that his Olympian travel schedule is necessary. Last December he struck a $950 million friendly merger deal with Telex and as chief executive of Memorex Telex he must now weld together a far-flung network of manufacturing, sales and service operations in 27 countries. When everything is nailed down, says Ronchi, he'll probably cut back to his 'normal' level of 150–200 travel days per year.

Psychologist Cooper argues that Ronchi 'could be a time bomb walking around. He may seem perfectly healthy, but the stress is taking its toll. And the heart disease caused by stress is cumulative.' Cooper also maintains that 'everybody needs some kind of social support system in their life, and we've found that the family is the best support system there is.' As for the reaction of his family, Ronchi says simply: 'I married an angel.' Nevertheless, he admits that constant travel is hard on his family.

Find the part of the article on the previous page which refers to the costs of too much travel. Then complete the tree diagram below with words from the text.

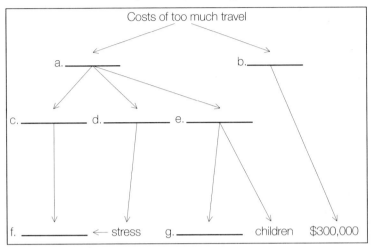

Costs of too much travel

a. _____

b. _____

c. _____ d. _____ e. _____

f. _____ ← stress g. _____ children $300,000

Text 4

Although most companies would certainly want their managers to travel a lot less than Giorgio Ronchi does, perhaps there are useful tips to get from his way of travelling.

He carries three thick airline schedules with him everywhere and is actively involved in putting together his own travel plans. 'No one else can really do it, because only I know all the right connections,' he explains. For example, he plans only 15 minutes to clear immigration in Atlanta, but counts on 90 minutes in New York. A 45 minute flight connection in Frankfurt is a piece of cake. A two-hour connection in Dallas is tight.

Ronchi travels with three lightweight suits and three changes of clothes. He never checks baggage, but limits himself to carry-on. He never buys duty-free goods, nor does he shop anywhere else. He books only aisle seats near the front of the aircraft in the no smoking section. Before buckling his seat belt, he removes his jacket, empties all its pockets and stows it away, one of the many small routines that distinguish the peripatetic business traveller from the amateur. Another indicator is the two-time-zone watch, with the normal clock face set at local time and a digital readout giving the time at his home office in Milan.

Ronchi then settles down to work. He never watches the movie or sleeps, unless he is on a long-haul flight and his normal bedtime is approaching. He also eats only about one-third of the food offered during the flight. He drinks plenty of liquids, but never alcohol. Because of this austere regimen, he doesn't miss the comforts of first class travel. Company policy dictates that all travel be economy (business) class.

After landing and clearing customs, Ronchi often has a business meeting at one of the growing number of airport business centres, especially in Europe, where stopovers don't add to the price of a ticket. Faxes, telexes and other messages may be waiting for him at the airport. If he's staying overnight, he collects his messages when he checks into his hotel, often an airport hotel. Also waiting for him will be a detailed schedule and itinerary for that evening and the next day, sent by his secretary in Milan.

Find all the recommendations (positive and negative) in the text and list them in this box.

DO	DON'T

Transfer 1

Task 9

Now look at three suggested paragraphs for a memo. Two are acceptable, one is not. Which is it?

a) When you book your flights, make sure you check with the Travel Section first. Many new independent airlines are operating flights that offer better service and flexibility than the 'national' airlines at lower cost.

b) Although business travel is a fact of life, too much of it can lead to difficulties later on for the manager and, therefore, for the company too. 120 days a year is generally thought to be the limit.

c) Conditions at US airports vary widely, affecting onward travel. For example, clearing immigration in New York normally takes four times as long as in Atlanta. Travel Section has constantly updated details of the situation at all major US airports. Check with us when you are planning your journey.

Transfer 2

Write a memo to middle and senior management containing some recommendations on travel arrangements for company employees. Include ideas based on the three texts in this unit.

Information Technology

Introduction

You have recently been sent from your company's Head Office to its United Kingdom subsidiary. You have to prepare a report on ways to increase productivity in the Electronic Data Processing (EDP) Department. You are particularly interested in ISDN (Integrated Services Digital Network) and new business software for senior managers.

The texts in this unit form part of your research. Read the following Key Words and the examples of their use which follow. Check the meaning of any words you do not know in a dictionary.

Key Words

subsidiary	productivity	counterpart
to vary	standalone	integrated
compatible	to dominate	to alleviate
wary	to claim	questionnaire
findings	proprietary	

- While the Group made a profit, some European **subsidiaries** reported a loss. In all sectors **productivity** improved.

- The largest telecommunications company in Spain, Telefónica, has considerably modernised its network in recent years. Its Italian **counterpart**, Societá Italiana Per l'Esercizio Telefonico, is doing the same but the quality of the service **varies** from one region to another.

- **Standalone** computers are by definition not **integrated** into a network.

- IBM **dominates** the mainframe and microcomputer market, having around 50%.

- Purchasing managers who want to **alleviate** the problem of users unable to communicate via computer should look for **compatible** equipment.

- Training is another problem and it is important to be **wary** of manufacturers who **claim** that learning to use their software takes 'only a few hours'.

- A **questionnaire** on computer use in European companies showed that there was a high degree of spending but low quality of use. These **findings** surprised the researchers.

- A **proprietary** product is one where the manufacturer has sole ownership of the patent, so no other manufacturer can produce a similar product, without a special licence.

Text 1

Task 1

In the magazine *Which Computer?* you find an article called 'The Screening of Britain' – a survey of how British business is making use of computers. This article is reproduced on the following page. The information given in the text is actually in three parts, indicated by particular words and by features of the layout or design of the text. Before looking for the key information, answer the following questions.

1 Where is the key finding of the research? Is it at the beginning, in the middle or at the end?
2 What phrase is used to introduce the key information?
3 What does '*startling*' mean (line 1)? a) obvious b) unexpected c) absurd? (Do not use a dictionary, the answer is in the opening two paragraphs of the text).
4 Which two phrases in the text indicate that you are going to read other findings?
5 What particular feature in the design or layout of the text is used to indicate findings from the research?

The Screening of Britain

One of the startling findings to emerge from a survey conducted by the National Computing Centre (NCC) is the extent to which the standalone micro-computer is being outnumbered by its better connected counterpart.

Other surprise findings in the survey show that:

• What is sometimes called 'end-user computing' is set to grow like wildfire in British companies during the next five years.

• Micros are already being heavily used for communicating with other machines.

• British companies have very heavy investments in computing facilities, with estimated average spends running at between £340 and £2,600 per employee per year depending on sector.

Detailed questionnaires were sent to 4,300 organisations, of which 20 per cent (845 organisations) replied. In terms of size, nearly 40 per cent of these employed fewer than 500 people, while a further third had between 1,000 and 5,000 employees. The survey was reasonably spread over industrial sectors and so claims to cover the broad spectrum of British industry.

The results were collated and analysed by Dominick Cornford of the NCC, an expert in the organisation of IT in business. He then met with our own writers, who spent a further few weeks studying the data and speaking to a number of the participants.

Based on this analysis, we also found out that:

• Senior managers are the fastest-growing category of new computer users.

• The IBM PC standard is rapidly consolidating its hold on UK corporate desktops, though not necessarily in the form of actual IBM machines.

• There are more micros connected to other services and more on local area networks than expected, and networked and communicating PCs are expected to increase faster than standalone machines.

• The dominant type of software provided with desktop micros is the spreadsheet.

• Two microcomputer packages – Lotus 1-2-3 and Ashton-Tate's dBase II and III – are still dominant as end-user applications packages. The inertia due to employees' investment in time and formatted data for these packages mean that competitors will have a hard time dislodging these market leaders.

Many of the organisations surveyed have a complete range of computing facilities from mainframes to desktop micros. On the big computer side, the survey found that IBM continues to dominate the market with 28.4 per cent of installed units (and a market share, by value, of around 50 %).

On the minicomputer front, IBM's dominance is much less marked. For systems costing less than £100,000 IBM had 365 sites in the sample, compared with DEC's 301 and ICL's 250.

Task 2

Scanning the numbers will often give you much of the most important information that the text contains. Scan the numbers in the extracts from the article to help you complete the notes below.

1 Organisations covered by the survey . . . .

2 Percentage of these with less than 500 employees . . . .

3 Percentage with 1000–5000 employees . . . .

4 Average UK spend per employee on computing . . . .

5 Dominant end user applications packages . . . .

6 IBM's market share of large computer market . . . .

7 IBM's share of the minicomputer market . . . .

69

Not all the important information in the text can be found by scanning for numbers. Read the text in more detail now and find the answers to the following questions.

1 The key finding of the research.
2 Five other findings.

Text 2

ISDNs are not in full commercial service yet. Skim the review below, from *Communications Management*, of the ISDN situation in Europe to help you complete the table on the following page and to inform you of the two main problems with ISDNs at present.

Tomorrow's network today? – European ISDN has stalled around the thorny problem of standards, while the national administrations go their own way with pilot services. Peter Purton reports.

The all-singing, all-dancing telecom network for the 21st century is here... well, almost.

Despite the number of European telecom administrations making claims like 'the first
5 commercial ISDN service', 'the first full-specification ISDN service', and 'the first published ISDN tariffs', real ISDN, based on real standards, is still some way off. There are probably no more than 3000 integrated services digital network (ISDN) users in Europe, and
10 the debatable definition of what constitutes an ISDN makes even this low figure a little shakey.

In the UK, for example, where British Telecom claims the first ISDN-like service with its Integrated Digital Access (IDA), not much attention has been paid to
15 standards. True, users can enjoy the benefits of taking just a few seconds to transmit a page of text on Group 4 digital facsimile terminals, super clear voice lines, video terminals allowing the transmission of proofs to printers and so on. However, instead of the standard 64 Kbit/s
20 plus 64 Kbit/s plus 16 Kbit/s channel configuration, BT's IDA uses a proprietary 64 Kbit/s plus 8 Kbit/s, plus 8 Kbit/s. There are also other major differences from international standards in such vital areas as signalling and physical interfaces.
25 The Deutsche Bundespost claims to be running the most extensive and international standards-compatible

ISDN trials to date, although these vary significantly from the declared international standard when it comes to looking at the transmission techniques used in the
30 local loop. Nevertheless some 800 users have been gradually connected to two ISDN pilot exchanges in Mannheim and Stuttgart since January 1988.

It is with the start of the fully commercial service this autumn, however, that West German users will really
35 have a chance to test ISDN's worth. Commercial ISDN exchanges are due to come into service in the country's eight major commercial centres. By the end of 1990 some 200 ISDN exchanges are planned to be in operation and by 1993 some 600 exchanges, or 20 per
40 cent of all local exchanges, are due to be ISDN.

France Telecom started its trials of ISDN in December 1987 and has set itself some of the most ambitious goals. The company has already launched a full commercial service based on these trials and is still
45 confident that it will meet its target of some 95,000 basic access ISDN subscribers by 1992. Spurred on by success with the Transpac public digital network and Teletel videotex network, France Telecom believes it can reach similar heights with ISDN.
50 There are two basic problems with ISDN, however. Continuous delays and disagreements have been a feature of the standards-setting process. But most importantly, pressure from users to encourage the development of ISDN by finding new and exciting
55 applications has not been as great as hoped for.

Country	System Code	Start date	Run by	Target
Britain		???		???
Germany				
France				

Problems: a) . . . .

b) . . . .

Task 5

Linking words tell you how sentences, or parts of sentences, are related to each other. They are signals that instruct you how to make sense of the text. Each of these signals has a meaning associated with it. The meanings of the most common linking words are shown in the box below.

because	reason, cause	if	condition
and	addition		
although however but nevertheless	contrast	for example for instance	example

Look through the article on the previous page to see how many examples of these linking words you can find and how they are used. Notice particularly how the four 'contrast' words are used in different positions.

Task 6

Use linking words from the list above to complete these sentences.

1 The product was old, ... it still sold very well.

2 The product was good, ... it still sold very well.

3 . . . . the product was good, it still sold very well.

4 . . . . the product was old, it still sold very well.

5 They have had trials for many years. The full commercial service,

. . . ., will not be started for some time.

6 They won't go bankrupt . . . . they can sell some assets.

Text 3

Software companies are now offering a new type of business program for management – 'decision support' software. Read the following article from *International Management* and make notes on the two programs described. Find the following key points for each program.

1 Program name
2 Produced by
3 Type
4 Basic units
5 Process

PRODUCTIVITY

THE HARD SELL FOR MANAGEMENT SOFTWARE

Gone are the days when personal computer software manufacturers merely offered to help managers become familiar with basic word processing and learn a couple of user friendly spreadsheet or graphics applications. Now software salesmen are making even more outlandish claims about how their computer programs can increase productivity, boost your memory and intellectual capabilities, and change your life generally.

The more grandiose the sales pitch, the more sceptical many senior executives become about the value of the latest wave of 'decision-support software' on offer. Managers have good reason to be wary. Many of these programs are poorly conceived and can be a waste of both time and money. But others really can change your life, or at least help you to plan and organise it more effectively.

'The programs must be very easy to manipulate yet complex enough to do a lot of different things,' says David Tebbut, a former ICL project manager turned software author. Tebbut's own product, called Brainstorm, is a sophisticated software 'ideas organiser' that is cheap, easy to use

and quite helpful. Brainstorm is essentially a flexible text-organiser that allows users to create and re-arrange 'thought maps' by entering text on a personal computer. Once entered, the text can later be structured and categorised at will. The program breaks up a large task into a series of small tasks, allowing you to solve them one at a time.

Perhaps the most ambitious bit of decision-support software yet seen on the market is Agenda, a program developed by Lotus Development Corp. of Cambridge, Massachusetts. Agenda is best described as a flexible free-form database program, although it represents an advance beyond the capabilities of many other database programs to be found on the market. Agenda, which supposedly runs on an IBM PC or compatible, organises written material into 'items' up to 350 characters long (about 58 words), and 'categories' or indexes of related items. In addition, a 'note' of 10K (10 written pages) can be attached to each item. Unlike nearly all other database programs, Agenda allows the user to begin typing in items and notes without setting up categories for them beforehand.

The bad news is that Agenda is not easy to learn. While computer-literate managers, engineers and secretaries may be able to get going fairly quickly on Agenda, those with little or no computer experience may come away from early sessions with migraines and shaky hands. Lotus knows this and is trying to alleviate problems caused by the program's complexity. The company formed a partnership last June with Time/system, a UK-based management consultancy that offers training seminars for floundering users in Europe and maintains a telephone 'hotline' to handle users' enquiries.

'This kind of training can be enormously expensive,' says Andrew Redfern, technical editor of *Personal Computer World*. 'If you aren't careful you can spend $500 a day on computer help. How many small to medium-sized companies are willing to do that?' Training is probably the key factor determining how many managers continue to use the new wave of business software. Unfortunately, the after-sales service and counselling provided by many software makers is woefully deficient.

© Copyright International Management

To avoid repeating themselves, writers often use synonyms (words with the same meaning). All of the words in the lists below are from the article on the previous page. Choose a synonym for each word on the left from the list on the right.

1	executives	a	to boost
2	sceptical	b	software
3	sophisticated	c	to manipulate
4	to increase	d	wary
5	to use	e	complex
6	programs	f	managers

Transfer

Task 9

Now that you have done the basic early reading for your report, write a memo to your Managing Director with your suggestions. Say what you think is the probable order of priority for the two areas you considered. When could each of them be implemented – in the short, medium or long term?

Economics

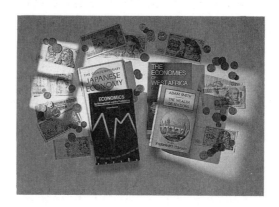

Introduction

You have been asked to produce a report on economic indicators and prospects in Asia. The first country you look at is Japan. The three texts in this unit form part of your research. Prepare notes for inclusion in your report on the following topics.

1 Comparison of recent economic indicators with other large industrial economies.
2 The status of R&D (Research & Development) in Japanese industry.
3 Prospects for the Japanese economy.

Task 1

Key Words

Study the following words. Use a good dictionary to help you. Write definitions for each word or phrase.

output	demand	housebuilding
wholesale prices	consumption	inflation
government spending	interest rates	growth
capital investment	outlook	prospects
patent	revenue	manpower
GDP (gross domestic product)		

Text 1

The following text, divided into three parts, is from the 'Economic and Financial Indicators' section of *The Economist*.

1 Read the text below on 'Output, Demand and Jobs' and use it to help you complete the gaps marked ❶, ❷, ❸ and ❹ in the table.
2 Write notes comparing the Japanese performance with a) the U.S.A. b) Germany.

ECONOMIC AND FINANCIAL INDICATORS

OUTPUT, DEMAND AND JOBS America's industrial production increased by 0.1% in April, the first monthly rise for seven months, but output was still 3.3% lower than a year ago. Retail sales in Germany soared by 10.9% in the 12 months to March. Australia's unemployment rose to 9.9% of its labour force in April, its highest level for 7½ years. In the same month Spain's jobless rate remained at 15.2% for the third consecutive month, Canada's fell to 10.2%, Sweden's edged down to 2.1% and Switzerland's rose to 1.1%.

% change at annual rate

	industrial production			GNP/GDP			retail sales [volume]			unemployment % rate		
	3 mths†	1 year		3 mths†	1 year		3 mths†	1 year		latest		year ago
Australia	+18.8	-0.1	Feb	+2.4	+0.6	Q4	-6.3	-1.6	Q4	❸	Apr	6.3
Belgium	+3.2	+5.0	Nov	na	+4.0	1989	-3.5	-0.8	Dec§	8.4	Mar*	8.0
Canada	-10.2	-6.0	Feb	-4.0	-1.0	Q4	-19.1	-15.2	Jan	❹	Apr	7.3
France	-0.3	+1.7	Feb	-1.6	+1.8	Q4	nil	-1.3	Feb	9.3	Mar	8.9
Germany	+8.6	+4.0	Mar	+1.5	+4.5	Q4	+23.6	❷	Mar	6.2	Apr	7.4
Holland	+17.0	+18.5	Feb	+13.7	+4.7	Q4	+2.2	+3.4	Dec§	4.9	Feb	5.3
Italy	-0.6	-2.2	Feb	+0.7	+1.1	Q4	+13.2	-4.2	Aug§	9.7	Mar	9.9
Japan	-0.8	+3.5	Mar	+2.1	+4.7	Q4	+1.9	+4.3	Jan	2.2	Mar	2.0
Spain	+0.2	+0.8	Feb	+3.4	+3.7	Q4	+8.4	+10.2	Dec§	15.2	Apr	15.7
Sweden	-1.3	-3.6	Feb	-0.6	-0.5	Q4	-1.2	+0.4	Jan	2.1	Apr*	1.1
Switzerland	-13.1	+1.8	Q4	-0.4	+1.7	Q4	-14.4	-0.8	Dec§	1.1	Apr*	0.5
UK	-5.8	-2.5	Feb	-3.8	-1.3	Q4	+3.2	+1.9	Mar	7.4	Mar	5.6
USA	-6.9	❶	Apr	-2.8	-0.6	Q4	-7.0	-3.5	Mar	6.6	Apr	5.4

§ Value index deflated by CPI. †Average of latest 3 months compared with avg. of previous 3 months, at annual rate.

1 Read the text below on 'Prices and Wages' and use it to help you complete the gaps marked ❶, ❷, ❸ and ❹ in the table.
2 Write notes comparing the Japanese performance with a) the USA b) Germany.

PRICES AND WAGES America's 12-month rate of consumer-price inflation remained at 4.9% in April; producer prices rose by 3.2% and wages increased by 3.3% – a real pay-cut of 1.5%. Australia's consumer-price inflation dropped to 4.9% in the year to March, its lowest level for six years. German workers received a 6.3% pay rise in the year to March, a real rise of 3.7% – the biggest in our table. Britain's producer prices increased by 6.4% in the year to April.

% change at annual rate

	consumer prices*			wholesale prices*			wages/earnings§		
	3 mths†	1 year		3 mths†	1 year		3 mths†	1 year	
Australia	-0.7	❶	Mar	+6.5	+5.1	Jan	+9.6	+6.3	Nov*
Belgium	+2.2	+2.9	Apr	-9.3	-1.3	Feb	+11.0	+5.3	Q2*
Canada	+12.1	+6.3	Mar	-0.4	+0.9	Mar	+9.3	+7.1	Feb
France	+1.9	+3.2	Mar	+4.6	+0.7	Q4	+4.8	+5.1	Jan*
Germany	+3.2	+2.8	Apr	+1.7	+1.8	Mar	+6.5	❹	Mar
Holland	+0.6	+2.6	Mar	-0.1	+0.8	Feb	+4.1	+2.6	Mar
Italy	+7.6	+6.7	Apr	+18.5	+8.1	Dec	+6.4	+7.1	Dec*
Japan	+2.0	+4.0	Mar	+0.4	+1.00	Mar	+7.0	+5.5	Feb
Spain	+4.1	+5.9	Apr	+1.2	+1.6	Mar	+2.7	+50.2	Q4
Sweden	+18.9	+10.7	Mar	+3.1	+3.1	Mar	+7.3	+4.4	Feb*
Switzerland	+7.6	+5.9	Apr	+1.2	-0.1	Mar	na	+5.2	Oct
UK	+2.4	+8.2	Mar	+8.5	+6.4	Apr	+11.4	+9.3	Feb
USA	+2.8	❷	Apr	-3.8	❸	Apr	+3.7	+3.3	Apr

§ Hourly wage rates in manufacturing except Australia, weekly earnings; Japan and Switzerland, monthly earnings; Belgium, Canada, Sweden and USA, hourly earnings UK, monthly earnings for all employees. † Average of latest 3 months compared with avg. of previous 3 months, at annual rate.

Task 4

Read the following text on 'Housebuilding' and then answer these questions.

1 Why is housebuilding a good indicator of economic activity?
2 Complete the labelling of the graph (a, b and c).
3 Make a note on the housebuilding in Japan compared with the U.S.A. and Germany.

HOUSEBUILDING A good leading indicator of economic activity is residential construction. As interest rates rise, housing starts fall, signalling a downturn; later, a revival of housing starts usually precedes the recovery. In all four countries shown in the chart, starts fell in the last quarter of 1990. In America, slow population growth means that housing starts have been falling for years. Even so, the figures show no end to the recession: starts fell by 36% during the past year, and are still dropping. Britain's figures, belying most other recent indicators, are less gloomy: though hugely down on 1988, its housing starts touched bottom months ago. Japan and Western Germany are in much better shape. Starts in both those countries are at levels close to those of a year earlier.

All figures seasonally adjusted except*

Western Germany: consolidated figures for Germany not yet available.

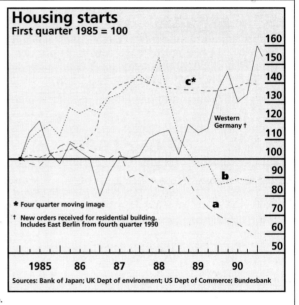

Housing starts
First quarter 1985 = 100

* Four quarter moving image
† New orders received for residential building. Includes East Berlin from fourth quarter 1990

Western Germany †

1985   86   87   88   89   90

Sources: Bank of Japan; UK Dept of environment; US Dept of Commerce; Bundesbank

Task 5

Many verbs in these three extracts from *The Economist* in this unit refer to trends or movements in figures.

1 Indicate below which of the given words mean to increase (),
to decrease (↘), and which means to stay the same (→).

to increase	to rise	to remain at
to drop	to fall	to edge down
to soar	to touch bottom	

2 Which two verbs are irregular? Give their complete paradigms (e.g. to begin, began, begun).
3 Explain in more detail what 'to edge down', 'to soar' and 'to touch bottom' mean. If you are not sure, look again at how they are used in the extracts.
4 Four of these verbs have an equivalent noun form. Which are they and what is it? Example: to increase (*v*), an increase (*n*).
5 Think of other verbs that could be included in this list. Do they have equivalent noun forms? If so, what are they?

Text 2

The text below consists of extracts from an article in a *Financial Times* survey on Japanese industry. Here are the first six paragraphs, and the last three. As stated in Unit 1, the key information in long articles can often be found at the beginning and at the end. Also included on the following page are the three graphs and the pie chart contained in the original article.

Task 6

Look at the text. Consider only the title, the highlighted sentence beneath the title and in particular the three graphs and the pie chart on the following page. What is the main message of the article?

LOW-COST CAPITAL

More than just cheap finance

R & D is a core activity for large Japanese companies

TO celebrate its fiftieth anniversary, Fujitsu, Japan's leading computer maker, built a palace of steel and glass: not a new headquarters; but a 20-storey, Y20bn engineering centre.

From the top floor of the building, completed two years ago in Kawasaki, near Tokyo, Mr Masaka Ogi, president of Fujitsu Laboratories, the company's research subsidiary, surveys a vast research and development site.

"We are spending 13 per cent of total revenues on research and development", he says. "That's very high. From the standpoint of current profits we should decrease this percentage but we are thinking of the future."

The sense that the company will provide whatever is necessary for R&D is pervasive among large Japanese groups. R&D is a core activity for large Japanese companies, bound into the process of management, manufacturing and marketing. The question is whether the financial conditions under which they operate encourage Japanese companies to be more positive about R&D than their western rivals. Put bluntly, can they raise capital more cheaply than their western competitors?

Broadly speaking, the answer in the past has been 'yes'. After the war, Japan built a tightly-regulated financial system designed to channel low-cost funds to industry. However, the advantage has probably shrunk in recent years due to financial deregulation. It may even have been eliminated – at least temporarily – by this year's crash in the Tokyo stock market.

However, other factors are at least as important in encouraging the expansion of R&D spending – a high-growth economy, corporate structures which spread risk, existence of keirets or industrial groupings, and the role of main banks.

The most important reason why Japanese companies may be more willing to entertain risk than US groups is their experience of high-speed growth: investments are much more likely to succeed in such an environment. Other conditions also encourage companies to undertake risky projects. One is the readiness of banks to act as main banks to a company, taking on a greater share of debt than a western bank might and often providing advice and sometimes even personnel.

Similarly, companies inside the same keiretsu often collaborate on new projects. Even outside keiretsu, co-operation is common – between large companies and their suppliers and customers, for example, government too plays a role –

encouraging companies invest in R&D by providing pump-priming funds to collaborative schemes.

It seems unlikely these elements will disappear from Japan. So even if average cost of capital is now similar to US levels, Japanese companies will still find it easier to earmark funds for R&D. As the Office of Technology Assessment, the US Congress concluded in a report this year:

"In sum a network of policies, practices and relationships acts to support heavy investment in long-term performance in Japanese industry by spreading risk."

Stefan Wagstyl

78

THE TECHNOLOGY RACE

As Japan invests more in research and development. . .

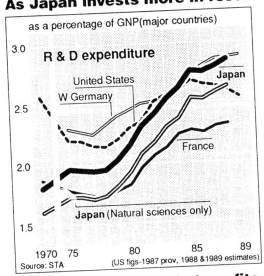

as a percentage of GNP(major countries)

R & D expenditure

United States
W Germany
Japan
France
Japan (Natural sciences only)

3.0
2.5
2.0
1.5

1970 75 80 85 89

Source: STA
(US figs-1987 prov, 1988 &1989 estimates)

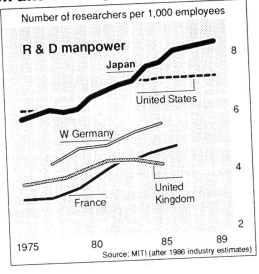

Number of researchers per 1,000 employees

R & D manpower

Japan
United States
W Germany
France
United Kingdom

8
6
4
2

1975 80 85 89

Source: MITI (after 1986 industry estimates)

. . . so the economic benefits flow

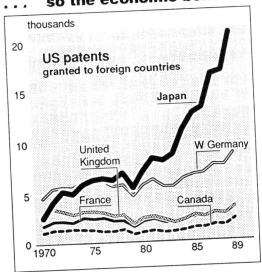

thousands

US patents
granted to foreign countries

Japan
United Kingdom
W Germany
France
Canada

20
15
10
5
0

1970 75 80 85 89

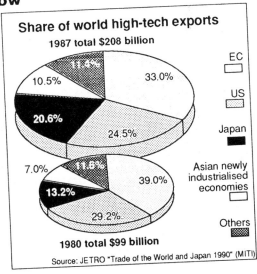

Share of world high-tech exports

1987 total $208 billion

11.4%
10.5%
33.0%
20.6%
24.5%

7.0%
11.6%
13.2%
39.0%
29.2%

1980 total $99 billion

EC
US
Japan
Asian newly
industrialised
economies
Others

Source: JETRO "Trade of the World and Japan 1990" (MITI)

79

Skim each paragraph and note the main idea (or possibly ideas) in each one. The first two are done for you.

Para. 1   50th anniversary - Fujitsu built ¥20 bn engineering centre.

Para. 2   Vast R + D site.

Para. 3

Para. 4

Para. 5

Para. 6

Para. 7

Para. 8

Para. 9

Text 3

Here are extracts from the beginning, the middle and the end of a report on Japan published by the Organisation for Economic Co-operation and Development (OECD).

Skim the text on the following page and complete this table by adding other items. An example of each is already given.

Factors having a positive effect on the economy	Factors with a potentially negative effect
high capacity utilisation	rise in rate of price increases

JAPAN

Key features

The economy continued to grow rapidly in 1990, sustained by strong business investment and buoyant private consumption. The current external surplus declined further. The
5 underlying rate of price increase appears to have risen, while remaining low, and as the labour market has tightened inflation fears have grown, prompting a more restrictive monetary policy. In response both to the
10 extraordinary strength of domestic demand and to the potential inflationary effect of the oil price rise …

… Recent surveys suggest that business investment may remain strong in the first part
15 of 1991, reflecting high levels of capacity utilisation and the incentive to substitute capital for labour because of persistant labour shortages. Real interest rates are projected to remain high, slowing the growth of
20 consumption and investment over the projection period. At the same time, continuing fiscal restraint is expected to result in a further increase in the general government surplus. Domestic demand may
25 thus decelerate to a more sustainable growth rate, and the unemployment rate may rise slightly. While the rate of inflation has increased in recent months, the effect of higher oil prices has been substantially offset
30 by the recent yen appreciation; the inflationary impulse should gradually subside in the following periods as the labour market and capacity utilisation rates ease. The current account surplus is projected to continue
35 declining over the projection horizon to some 1 per cent of GNP.

Recent trends

The economy is still operating at high levels of capacity utilisation. Real GNP grew at an annual rate of 7.4 per cent in the first half of
40 1990, with final domestic demand expanding at 7 per cent. Industrial production, which had stagnated from the third quarter of 1989, rebounded from the second quarter of 1990. Labour market conditions are generally still
45 tight, and the ratio of job offers to job-seekers remains high. The annual year-on-year inflation rate (measured by the consumer price index excluding fresh food) fell to just over two per cent …

Prospects

50 The major forces shaping the short-term outlook are: i) the tightening of monetary conditions and the associated fall in share prices; ii) a further gradual increase in the general government surplus; iii) an OECD
55 average oil import price of $27 in the second semester of 1990, remaining unchanged in real terms thereafter; and iv) a slowdown in the growth of world trade, though it picks up towards the end of the projection horizon.

81

The text on the previous page shows several cause and effect relationships. For example, the first sentence tell us '*The economy continued to grow rapidly in 1990, sustained by strong business investment and buoyant private consumption*'. This can be represented as follows:

Strong business investment

+

buoyant private consumption ➤ growth of the economy

Complete the following flow diagrams to show cause and effect relationships.

1. labour market has tightened ➤ a ....

                                        b ....

2. .... ➤ capital substituting labour.

3. a .... ➤ government surplus,

                                        b ....

                                        and

                                        c ....

Certain words are commonly used to express cause and effect relationships. The text on the previous page contains examples. These, and others, are given in the box below.

prompting (line.8)

because of (17)

to result in (22-23)

thus (25)

to cause

to lead to

due to

Complete the paragraph below by adding an appropriate form of any of
the words or phrases in the box on the previous page. Two are done for
you as examples.

Inflation is (1). *caused*. . . . . .by high consumption, high public spending and
high wage increases. In the early 1990s rising inflation (2). . . . . the U.K.
government to increase interest rates. Some companies closed (3). . . . .
debts and high costs of borrowing. (4). *Thus* . . . . .the higher interest rates
(5). . . . . .higher unemployment. Since high inflation can
(6). . . . . .an economy losing competitiveness, the government felt
that it was necessary to suffer higher unemployment. However, government spending
also rose (7). . . . . .unemployment.

Note
The verb '*to result in*' is always followed by either a noun phrase or a verb in the
gerund (-*ing* form), or a combination of both (noun + gerund). Examples: Wrong
decisions can result in serious consequences. Inflation always results in an economy
losing strength.

Task 11

Look at the context in which these words from the text on page 81 are used, then
decide which word or phrase on the right means the same.

sustained by (line 2)	a) helped by b) causing c) making necessary
buoyant (3)	a) low b) high c) modern
further (4)	a) a little b) a long way c) more
prompting (8)	a) helping b) producing c) stopping
domestic demand (10)	a) consumer spending b) political problems c) shortage of goods
capacity utilisation (15-16)	a) closing factories b) new factories c) factories producing maximum possible
labour shortages (17-18)	a) strikes b) jobs on offer, few workers to do them c) unemployment
interest rates (18)	a) inflation b) cost of borrowing c) high wages
fiscal restraint (22)	a) high taxation b) high government spending c) low taxation and low government spending
surplus (24, 54)	a) strength b) money available c) debts
thus (25)	a) later b) this c) in this way
slightly (27)	a) a lot b) a little c) quickly
offset (29)	a) increased b) represented c) cancelled out
appreciation (30)	a) increased value b) stability c) devaluation

The following verbs all occur in the text on page 81. Find them and make sure you understand what they mean.

to grow (lines 1, 8, 38)	to rebound (43)	to ease (33)
to rise (6, 26)	to remain unchanged (56)	to stagnate (42)
to remain high (19)	to decline (4, 35)	to fall (48)
to decelerate (25)	to remain strong (14)	to pick up (58)
to subside (31)	to slow (19)	
to expand (40)	to increase (23)	

Transfer 1

Task 13

You are now ready to start your report for the Managing Director. Which of the following sentences would you use in it?

1 Japanese GDP has increased in the last year at a similar rate to Germany and the United States.
2 Consumer spending in the last year in Japan is much higher than in the United States but much lower than in Germany.
3 Unemployment is very low in Japan compared with almost all large industrialised countries.
4 The construction industry in Japan is in good shape.
5 R&D is a central activity for Japanese companies.
6 Japan has almost 50% of the world's high tech exports.
7 Prospects for the Japanese economy show a gradual increase in government surplus.

Transfer 2

Write a report on the Japanese economy based on the information you have found in this unit. You may like to include other information based on other articles in this book or your own knowledge and experience.

Transfer 3

Find some financial documents and journals in English relevant to your work, especially ones dealing with recent performance and prospects.

1 Skim a text to find the main ideas and general meaning.
2 Look at any graphs or other diagrams.
3 Finally, read the text in detail to see how the financial changes are described, particularly movements up and down.

unit 10

Company Accounts

Introduction

This unit looks at profit and loss accounts, and balance sheets. They can be used by the public, employees, suppliers, potential business partners, investors, banks and other credit institutions to judge the financial strength of a company. The texts are extracts from *The Annual Accounts* by W.P. Ridley in *The Gower Handbook of Management*.

Imagine that you are a director of a company which is considering a partnership with Pangloss PLC, the company which is the subject of the texts in this unit. There are two options, either your company enters a joint venture with Pangloss, or you make a takeover bid – an attempt to buy the company. Your board of directors has asked you to examine the finances of Pangloss PLC and to make your recommendation.

The words and phrases in the Key Words section on the following page are all concerned with finance and accounts. Check you understand them. Use a dictionary, if necessary.

Key Words

creditors
balance sheet
dividend
fixed assets
current assets
to lend
ordinary share capital
freehold land & buildings

loss
materials
mortgage debenture
profit
profit & loss account
recipient
to judge
shares

loan
wages
liabilities
depreciation
opening stock
cost of sales

Task 1

Explain the words in italics in the sentences below.

1 The company announced a *dividend* of DM 0.67 per *share*.
2 Before agreeing to *lend* money, banks always examine the financial situation and prospects of the potential borrower.
3 If a borrower cannot repay a *loan*, the bank may insist on the sale of any *freehold land and buildings* or recover the value of the loan from other *assets*.
4 When a company goes bankrupt, or ceases trading, *liabilities* are met, as far as possible, out of assets.

Task 2

Complete the sentences below with a word or phrase from the above list of Key Words.

1 . . . . are people or companies to whom the company owes money.
2 . . . . is goods held by the company at the start of the financial year.
3 The . . . . is a statement of the assets and liabilities of the company on a specified date.
4 The . . . . .shows the financial activities, both in terms of money received or owed, and money paid or owed, for a given period.
5 . . . . are assets held for use by the company, not for resale.
6 . . . . are assets temporarily held by the company, such as cash or stock.
7 When a company makes a capital investment, for example – it buys machinery – the cost is spread over the projected useful life of the item. This is called . . . .
8 . . . . includes the cost of materials, wages, production costs, etc.
9 The total amount of money invested in a company in exchange for . . . . is called the . . . .

Text 1

Well-organised text helps understanding. Similarly, recognising how a text is organised can help you. In the following text, the first paragraph explains the contents of the section. The next paragraph begins by introducing an important element in P&L accounts. The rest of the paragraph explains why it is important. Skim the text and note the following key points.

1 The subject of this section.
2 What important element is the subject (or topic) of the second paragraph?
3 What important element is the subject (or topic) of the third paragraph?

PROFIT AND LOSS ACCOUNT FOR PANGLOSS PLC

This chapter takes the abridged accounts of a company called Pangloss PLC to highlight information on which a financial examination is based (see Figure 1).

In the year to 31 March 1985 Pangloss earned £1.4m before a charge of £0.4m for depreciation; depreciation is singled out because it does not represent a direct cash outflow but an accounting adjustment to the value of fixed assets – some of which are likely to have been bought many years before. Therefore when considering the cash resources available to the company both the level of depreciation and retained profits will be taken into account. The trading surplus net of depreciation gives pre-interest profits – an important indicator of company trading performance – of £1.0m.

Interest charge

The interest charge depends on the amount of loans and overdrafts outstanding, which is an integral part of the financing of the company's assets, rather than of current trading. It is therefore of prime significance to those providing finance whether as lenders or investors. From the point of view of a potential lender, the relation of the interest charge to the level of pre-interest profits gives some indication of the security for loans; in this case with interest at £0.3m he is likely to be deterred by the relatively high ratio of 30 per cent of pre-interest profits (of £1m) already absorbed by interest.

YEAR TO 31 MARCH 1985

		£m
	Trading surplus (before depreciation)	1.4
Less:	Depreciation	0.4
	Pre-interest profits	1.0
Less:	Interest	0.3
	Pre-tax profits	0.7
Less:	Tax	0.3
	Available to shareholders	0.4

Fig 1. Abbreviated profit and loss account of Pangloss PLC

Detailed understanding. Read the text on the previous page again. Why are the two elements featured in paragraphs 2 and 3 so important? In the original text, paragraph 3 continues with an example showing the effects of the £0.3m interest charges on a 70% increase in sales, or on a 70% fall in sales. Do these calculations yourself. Then say what you think are the implications of interest payments of £0.3m for prospective lenders.

Text 2

Pre-reading

Another section of the Profit and Loss account which is very important in judging the financial strength of a company is the '*return on shares*'. If you are not sure what this means, skim the text entitled '*Return to Shareholders*' on the following page, and try to guess what '*return on shares*' means.

The return on shares is judged by looking at earnings and dividends. Earnings per share (e.p.s.) is calculated by dividing the profit for the year by the number of shares issued. It represents the total earnings, including dividends. Dividends are extra payments from profit which the directors of the company distribute to shareholders.

Shareholders and prospective shareholders naturally consider the return on shares with interest. The text below deals with this section of the profit and loss account.

Now read the text on the following page, but do not try to understand every word. Just skim the text and answer these questions.

1 Should prospective investors buy Pangloss shares at £2?
2 What advice would you give to someone who was considering buying Pangloss shares?

RETURN TO SHAREHOLDERS

Earnings of £0.4m on 2 million shares (see Figure 2) are equivalent to 20p per share in Pangloss. The value of the share is normally directly related to this figure; thus, if the share price is £2 an investor will consider whether it is reasonable to buy or sell the share given that £2 is equivalent to ten times the earnings attributable to that share (that is a p/e ratio of 10). The dividend must also be considered – for long-term investors, this represents the direct return. At a price of £2 the dividend of 10p per share represents a 5 per cent net return on the investment; because tax is already deducted, the dividend is free of tax up to the standard rate in the hands of the recipient. The 5 per cent return is therefore worth 7.0 per cent in gross terms to the standard taxpayer at current rates of tax. Better returns are offered by an investment in gilts. The investor has therefore to judge whether the trading prospects of Pangloss offer scope for this dividend to be steadily increased.

YEAR ENDED 31 MARCH 1985

Earnings for the year to 31.3.85 = £0.4m or 20p per share*
Recommended dividend   = £0.2m or 10p per share*

Retained profits   = £0.2m

*Issued capital 2 million ordinary shares of £1

Fig 2. Earnings, dividends and retentions of Pangloss PLC

Task 6

Find words or expressions in the text which mean approximately the same as these words.

1 a person who puts their money into a company, hoping to make a profit
2 advisable
3 many months or years
4 after tax
5 taken off
6 normal
7 person who receives something
8 before tax
9 investments in government securities (government stocks and bonds)
10 assess
11 future business
12 potential
13 regularly

Text 3

Pre-reading

Another factor which helps in judging the financial strength of a company is the total value of its shares and the amount of money a company borrows from banks. Before reading the text, how much do you think a company could reasonably borrow against its total value as security?

Task 7

Scan the balance sheet on the following page (just the figures, not the text). Find the following information.

1 How much Pangloss is borrowing?
2 How much the company is worth?

Task 8

The text above the balance sheet comments on the situation you have considered in Task 7. Before you read the text, decide what you think it will say, and try to answer the following questions.

1 Do you think Pangloss is in a very strong position?
2 Do you think Pangloss could borrow more money?
3 Do you think investors are likely to invest more money in the company?

Now skim the text to check your answers to these three questions.

Task 9

Detailed understanding. Answer the following questions. If you are not sure of the meaning of some of the expressions, try to guess it from the context; i.e. given the other words in the sentence or paragraph, what is the probable meaning of the word or words you don't know. If the context does not help, or you have no idea, use a dictionary to check the meaning of some of the words.

1 How is the 'book value' of the shares calculated?
2 According to the balance sheet, what would happen to the assets of Pangloss if the company went into liquidation?
3 Explain 'scope for raising funds'.
4 What two things does a potential lender consider?
5 Explain 'ability to service the interest charge out of current profits'.
6 Explain 'the asset backing for loans'.
7 Explain '4 per cent debenture'.
8 Explain 'falls to be redeemed'.
9 How are the 'funding problems of Pangloss clearly likely to discourage investors'?

BALANCE SHEET FOR PANGLOSS PLC

Value of shares

The first point of interest raised by the balance sheet is the book value of the shares. Of the £11m capitol employed in Pangloss at the end of the year, £6m is shown to be financed by shareholders' funds giving a book value of £3 each for the 2m shares. (This allows for the assets of the company fetching the £11m shown and thus providing £6m surplus after paying off the debt finance of £5m).

Scope for raising funds

Secondly the balance sheet gives an indication of the scope of raising further finance. In this case with borrowing at £5m against £11m capitol employed, it is unlikely that leaders would be interested in advancing further funds to Pangloss. In addition to checking the company's ability to service the interest charge out of current profits, lenders are concerned with the asset backing for loans. It is rare for a company to obtain half its funds from borrowing. Within the £5m debt the £3m 4 per cent debenture explains the relatively low interest charge given in the profit and loss account. However, since it falls to be redeemed in 1986, it can be considered, with the bank overdraft, as short-term finance; the refinancing of the debenture could well be a rate of interest of 10 per cent instead if 4 per cent, increasing the interest charge by £180 000 from £120 000 to £300 000. Thus the funding problems of the Pangloss Company are clearly likely to discourage investors; for shareholders will expect to be asked to contribute further equity finance.

		£M
Sources of finance		
Share capital 2 million shares of £1		2
Retained profits		4
		—
		6
Shareholders' funds		
Debt finance		
4% Debenture 1986	3	
Bank overdraft	2	5
	—	
		11
Total funds		
Assets Employed		
Fixed assets	5	
Property	1	
Machinery	1	7
Vehicles	—	4
Net current assets		
		11
Total assets		

Fig 3. Abbreviated 1986 balance sheet for Pangloss PLC

Transfer 1

Write a short report to your board of directors on the financial strength of Pangloss PLC based on the information contained in the three extracts in this unit. Include some comments on the following:

- sales
- depreciation
- interest charges
- return to shareholders
- share value
- the company's need for extra funds, and the possibility of raising them.

Finally, make your recommendation on whether your company should enter a joint venture with Pangloss, or stage a takeover bid.

Transfer 2

Find a recent copy of the profit and loss account and the balance sheet for a company you are familiar with. Examine them to judge the financial strength of the company involved. Look in particular at some of the points from annual accounts studied in this unit.

 **Financial Planning**

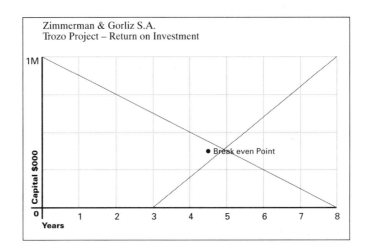

Zimmerman & Gorliz S.A.
Trozo Project – Return on Investment

Introduction

This unit looks at financial planning through the preparation of a master budget. This is the projected plan for revenue (income) and costs for a given period. It contains a budgeted income statement and a budgeted balance sheet. These are prepared by amalgamating individual budgets for various departments within the organisation.

The three texts are taken from 'The Master Budget and the Cash Budget' in *Accounting for Management Decisions* and include extracts from the master budget of one company, Somerton Ltd., for the year ending 31st December 1991.

Imagine you are the Financial Director of a medium-sized company. You have to present a report to the other directors on what is required in a master budget. The three texts will help you collect information for your report. Read them with two questions in mind, firstly, what considerations need to be made when compiling a master budget? Secondly, how useful is the Somerton Ltd. master budget?

Check that you understand the Key Words on the following page, all of which are common in describing financial planning. If you are not sure what they mean, try Task 1 before looking in a dictionary.

Key Words

allocation	gross	raw materials
budget	liquidity	demand
cash	net	expenditure
cash flow	overheads	unit
commission	profitability	variable
debtor	cost of sales	selling costs

Task 1

The following are nine definitions from *The English Business Dictionary*. Each one relates to one of the Key Words introduced above. Choose one of the words and match it to the correct definition. Then, using a dictionary, find definitions for the other eight words.

1 (adj)   total or with no deductions . . . .

2 (noun)   cash which comes into a company from sales less the money which goes out in purchases or overhead expenditure . . . .

3 (noun)   dividing a sum of money in various ways . . . .

4 (noun)   money in coins or notes . . . .

5 (noun)   need for goods at a certain price . . . .

6 (noun)   plan of expected spending and income . . . .

7 (noun phrase) substances which have not been manufactured (such as wool, wood, sand) . . . .

8 (noun)   a person who owes money . . . .

9 (noun phrase) all the costs of a product sold, including manufacturing costs and the staff costs of the production department. . . . .

Text 1

Pre-reading

Together with the master budget, you receive various component budgets: sales, production, raw materials, manufacturing overheads, cost of goods sold, capital expenditure budget, general and administrative budget, cash budget. All these are summarised in the budgeted income statement and balance sheet, or master budget. Text 1 on page 96 contains a description of some of the main points involved in compiling a sales budget, together with an example from Somerton Ltd.

Task 2

Remember that when you need particular information in a long text, you should look for particular words in the text. They will indicate where you can find the information you need. Use this technique to decide which paragraph deals with the following points.

1 factors affecting sales volume
2 factors affecting pricing policy
3 sales forecasts for Somerton Ltd
4 sales forecasting procedures
5 selling costs

Task 3

Scan the text to find the following information.

1 Somerton Ltd's estimated volume of sales (no. of units).
2 Somerton Ltd's unit price for Product Y.
3 Somerton Ltd's unit price for Product Z.
4 Somerton Ltd's estimated total value of sales.
5 Level of commission paid to Somerton Ltd salesmen.
6 Advertising/promotions budget.
7 Estimated total selling costs.

Note that for this exercise it is not necessary to read the whole text. Where can you find all this information?

Task 4

Detailed understanding. Find answers to the following questions.

1 What is the principal factor which affects volume of sales?
2 Name another factor which would presumably affect sales for a ski equipment manufacturer.
3 How can the level of non-regular business be included in sales forecasting?
4 What is the advantage of including senior management opinion in sales forecasting?
5 Why, if the production costs are the same, does the selling price sometimes differ between two items?

Sales Budget

a) The Sales Budget for an organisation is derived from estimates of the demand for (and the ability to supply) its different products at particular prices. These estimates are, in turn, determined on the basis of sales forecasts. Thus sales forecasting precedes sales budgeting.

b) The purpose of sales forecasting is to estimate the organisation's sales revenue for the budget period. Two interdependent factors make up sales revenue: the volume of sales and the selling price(s) – we examined the relationships between the two in Chapter 9. Some of the variables which may affect the organization's pricing policy are:

   (i) Extent of market competitions
   (ii) General economic and industrial conditions
   (iii) Organizational cost structure

c) Sales volume will be determined both by the chosen pricing policy and by some or all of the following additional factors:

   (i) Level of advertising and other promotional policies
   (ii) Quality of the sales force
   (iii) Past sales volume
   (iv) Any seasonal influences

d) The sales forecaster might use the above variables to predict first the level of regular business, comprising contracts already placed and the normal demand of regular customers; second, the level of non-regular business, comprising the likely demand from new customers and other non-repetitive sources (i.e. although certain individual transactions may not be repeated regularly, the total amount of such business may be stable from year to year) and finally the level of unstable business or unexpected demand which, by its very nature, is difficult to forecast.

e) Sales forecasting procedures can be very sophisticated and a detailed discussion of them lies outside the scope of this text. However, we note below some approaches that a forecaster might use in deriving his expectations.

   (a) *Assessments by sales department staff:* Estimates of sales demand might be made by the individual salesmen and subsequently be passed upwards for consideration by the sales managers. This approach has the advantage that individual salesmen can offer advice on the basis of detailed knowledge of the particular factors peculiar to their own areas.

   (b) *Mathematical analysis of past sales figures:* The purpose of such an analysis, of whatever degree of sophistication, is to indicate trends of the relationship between selling price and quantity demanded and, where possible, patterns of seasonal variation. This information can then be adjusted for known factors, such as the level of future advertising or changes in the degree of market competition, to produce future sales forecasts.

   (c) *Senior management judgement:* The meeting of the senior management team, which might include representatives of production management, purchasing and administration, as well as senior sales executives, may bring a wider variety of expertise to the forecasting exercise.

f) On the basis of sales forecasts we can draw up the sales budget for Somerton Ltd. as per Table 1. Note that although the 'conventionally' calculated production cost of the two products is the same (£7.50) their selling prices differ. This is a common occurrence in practice. It may result from certain products being advertised more heavily than others, from difference in the competitiveness of markets in which different products are sold, or from differences between the relevant incremental costs of products even though their costs calculated according to normal accounting conventions are the same.

Table 1 Somerton Ltd: Sales budget for the year to 31st December 1991			
	Units to be sold	Price (£)	Total sales revenue (£)
Product Y	40,000	10.00	400,000
Product Z	16,000	12.50	200,000
			£600,000

g) When the sales budget has been prepared, it is a relatively straightforward task to estimate the appropriate selling and distribution costs, i.e. those costs which depend upon the level of sales. The make-up of the selling expenses budget is shown in Table 2. Of the items making up the selling expenses budget only sales commission (5% of £600,000) varies directly with sales revenue; the remainder of the costs are fixed for the following year, although their actual amounts are, to a large extent, determined by the expected volume of sales.

Table 2 Somerton Ltd: Selling expenses budget for the year to 31st December 1991	
	£
Sales commission – 5% (£600,000)	30,000
Salaries	27,000
Travelling expenses	15,000
Advertising and promotion	23,000
	£95,000

Text 1

Text 2

Pre-reading

Another component of the master budget is the cash budget. The following text is about cash budgets and it is an example from Somerton Ltd. Before reading the text, explain what a cash budget is.

Task 5

Scan the following text and find this information.

1 the expected turnover for the year
2 the largest area of expenditure (i.e. the largest costs)
3 the total costs
4 the balance carried to the next year

The Cash Budget

Having prepared detailed budgets for each of the functional aspects of the business, we now draw up one of the most important budgets of all – the cash budget. The ability of the firm to generate cash flow represents its ability to pay dividends, and to succeed and grow in the future. The preparation of the cash budget aids management in its planning and in its desire to minimise unwanted, and non-productive, cash balances, while at the same time ensuring that, wherever possible, expensive borrowing to overcome short-term deficiencies is not incurred. Most organisations draw up their cash budgets on, at least, a monthly basis, and we will show how this can be done in the concluding section of this chapter; for the purposes of determining the Master Budget of Somerton Ltd. We show simply the total cash amounts for the full year. We assume in our analysis that debtors (amounts owed by customers) will increase over the year by £6,000, and that creditors (amounts owed to suppliers) for raw materials will increase by £5,000. Finally, we assume no other outstanding liabilities exist at 31st December 1991. The cash budget for the year is shown in Table 3.

Table 3 Somerton Ltd: Cash budget for the year to 31st December 1991

	£
Opening cash balance (per opening balance sheet)	22,500
Add Receipts	
Collections from customers	
(sales less £6,000 increase in debtors)	594,000
Total cash available	616,500
Less Payments	
for materials	
(purchases less £5,000 increase in creditors)	111,000
for selling expenses	95,000
for direct labour	171,000
for manufacturing overhead*	132,500
for capital equipment	35,000
for general expenses	65,000
Total cash needed	609,500
Closing cash balance	7,000

*Note that the cash payment for manufacturing overheads excludes the depreciation expense of £10,000, as depreciation is a non-cash item.

From the information given in the text on the previous page, answer the following questions.

1 Why is cash flow important?
2 Why is the cash budget important?
3 What is the usual time scale of a cash budget?
4 What is the time scale of the cash budget for Somerton Ltd. included here?
5 Is depreciation included? If not, why not?

Task 7

Find words in the text which mean approximately the same as the following.

1 companies who owe Somerton Ltd money
2 companies to whom Somerton Ltd owes money
3 money owed by Somerton Ltd
4 the arrival of money from customers
5 quantities of money not invested but held by the company
6 not having enough money for immediate needs
7 a notional sum of money representing loss of value in capital equipment

Text 3

Pre-reading

Before reading the text on the following page, think again about the following points.

• what a master budget contains
• what each part represents
• the purpose of a master budget

This text offers final comments on the compilation and use of master budgets, together with the example from Somerton Ltd.

Task 8

Remember that when you want to understand the main points in a text, it is not necessary to read the text in detail, or to try to understand everything. Skim the text and answer the following questions.

1 What are the main ways managers could use the master budget?
2 What are the limitations of the Somerton Ltd. master budget?
3 How is cost of goods sold calculated?

Summary of the Master Budget

The budgeted income statement and balance sheet represent the summarised plans for the whole organisation for the forthcoming period.

Certain decisions and inferences might be made by top management on the basis of the projected figures. For example, management might calculate certain key ratios to determine whether the position revealed by the budgeted statements is satisfactory. *Profitability* ratios would examine the relationships between net income and turnover, and net income and capital employed. Focus on Somerton Ltd's *liquidity* situation would question whether the projected cash balance is adequate, whether the debtors are likely to pay on time, whether the stocks of finished goods and work-in-progress are likely to prove saleable, whether the relationship between the totals of fixed assets and current assets is satisfactory, and whether the current assets/current liabilities ratio is optimal. Attention to the funds employed by the business might query the rationale of *financing* operations without any debt capital.

The two budgeted statements as we have presented them are static, deterministic budgets. They show the projected results of operating only at a single expected level of activity. They should be interpreted with caution, as it is unlikely that the firm will operate at exactly the level of activity embodied in the budgets. For control purposes it is imperative, as explained in the previous chapter, that the management supports the fixed master budget with a series of flexible budgets showing the expected results of operating at different levels of activity, and perhaps also with budgets showing, for example, the effects of changes in input and output prices.

In addition the conventions used to prepare the budgeted accounts are those commonly applied to the preparation of accounts for publication. For example, cost of goods sold includes allocated fixed costs and a charge for using fixed assets (a depreciation charge) based on an allocation of the original cost of assets. Hence, as we explained in Chapter 6 and subsequently, the figure for cost of goods sold may be a poor approximation to the expected relevant, opportunity cost of the goods to be sold. As an indication of what Somerton Ltd's published accounts will look like if actual performance for the year accords with budgeted performance, the budgeted income statement and balance sheet are satisfactory. However, insofar as they are used as a basis for preparing more detailed operating budgets, care must be taken to ensure that proper attention is paid to the sort of decision rules we have discussed in previous chapters.

Table 4 Somerton Ltd.:   Budgeted income statement and balance sheet

	£	£
Budgeted income Statement for the year to 31st December1991		
Sales		600 000
Less cost of goods sold		420 000
Gross profit		180 000
Less selling expenses	95 000	
General and administrative expenses	65 000	160 000
Budgeted net income		20 000
Budgeted Balance sheet as at 31st December 1991		
Fixed assets (net)		285 000
Current assets		
Stocks: Finished goods	15 000	
Work-in-progress	8 000	
Raw materials	7 000	
	30 000	
Debtors (£24 000 + £6 000)	30 000	
Cash	7 000	
	67 000	
Less Creditors (£12 000 + £5 000)	17 000	
Net current assets		50 000
Total net assets		£335 000
Represented by		
Issued share capital		240 000
Retained income as 1st January 1991		75 000
Budgeted net income for the year		20 000
Total long term funds		335 000

Task 9

Scan the table and find answers to the following questions.

1 What is the turnover Somerton Ltd. expects for the year ending 31st December 1991?
2 What is the gross profit?
3 What are the total forecasted expenses?
4 What is the net income?
5 What are the total net assets?
6 What is the composition of net fixed assets?

Transfer 1

On the basis of the three extracts you have read, compile a short report on what is required in a Master Budget.

Transfer 2

What elements in the preparation of a master budget are you involved with in your company? Take an example of either a master budget or a departmental budget and write a brief summary on how it was compiled (something similar to one of the texts used in this unit).

unit 12

Legal Contracts

Introduction

In this unit we look at some of the special problems of reading legal contracts. The language of contracts is often complicated by specialist vocabulary and long sentences. Study the following list of words common in legal contracts. Use your dictionary to check you understand them.

Key Words

to allege	joint participation	duration
amendment	join venture agreement	terms of a contract
to be defined as	to make a claim against	obligation
to be entitled to	to enter into an agreement	territory
to be in force	on the part of	to furnish
to claim	party/parties	to undertake
consent	prior	hereby
to default	solely	
delivery	to stipulate	

Task 1

Now explain the underlined words in the sentences below.

1 Lin Ltd and Wait & Co signed a contract
   entering into a joint venture to manufacture teapots.
2 The agreement stipulated that Lin would supply technical
   experts experienced in the design of teapots.
3 Under the terms of the contract Wait would not attempt to sell
   any teapots produced solely by them, without the prior consent
   of Lin.
4 To do so would represent a default on the part of Wait, and
   Lin would be entitled to demand an explanation.
5 In the event of such a default, Lin could make a claim against
   Wait, alleging the breaking of an agreement still in force.
6 Wait claimed that an amendment had been made to the original
   contract, permitting them to sell a particular teapot.
7 The two parties are now engaged in a legal dispute.
8 Meanwhile, Wait has given an undertaking not to proceed with
   sales of the teapot.

Text 1

Task 2

Notice the structure of the extract from a legal contract which appears on the following page. Skim the text and answer the following questions.

1 What part of the document is this?
2 What is the contract about?
3 What is the function of the following paragraphs?
   • paragraph one
   • paragraph two
   • paragraph three

Joint Venture Agreement

<u>This</u> agreement is entered into <u>this</u> 28th day of June 1991, by and between Fornaro Elettrica S.p.A., a company organised and existing under the laws of Italy, having its principal office at Alba, Cuneo, (hereinafter referred to as '<u>F</u>') and Warwick Photographic, a company organised and existing under the laws of Canada, having <u>its</u> principal office of Ottowa, Ca., (hereinafter referred to as '<u>W</u>').

WITNESSETH THAT

WHEREAS, '<u>F</u>' has acquired valuable experience, technical data and know-how relating to the designing, manufacturing, assembling and marketing of products defined as JWS-20.

WHEREAS, <u>the parties</u> recognising that they could only with difficulty separately and successfully exploit <u>such</u> business, agree that the most appropriate manner for <u>them</u> to enter into <u>said</u> business while minimising the technical and financial risks, is through <u>their</u> joint participation in the manufacture of <u>products</u>.

Task 3

An important element in understanding texts, and legal documents in particular, is to see the relationships between words in sentences. This is referencing.
Here is an example from the beginning of a Joint Venture Agreement.

<u>This</u> agreement is entered into on 17th March 1991 between Eurolectric of Hull and Pekka Oy of Helsinki. The <u>aforementioned parties</u> undertake to form a joint partnership to design, manufacture and market a printer. The <u>said product</u> shall bear the name of both participants in the <u>present</u> contract.

The underlined words in the paragraph at the bottom of the previous page refer to other words in the same paragraph.

this	refers to	'agreement'
aforementioned parties	refers to	'Eurolectric and Pekka'
said product	refers to	'printer'
both	refers to	'Eurolectric and Pekka'

Look at the first Joint Venture Agreement extract at the top of the previous page again. Decide what the underlined words refer to.

Text 2

Pre-reading

Task 4

The text on the following page is a copy of a Letter of Preliminary Agreement. Read the questions below, then scan the text to find the answers.

1 What is the purpose of the agreement?
2 Who are the parties involved?
3 What is the product?
4 How long is the agreement for?
5 What are the responsibilities of each party?
6 Who pays the expenses?

Letter of Preliminary Agreement

PASCUAL RUIZ CABESTANY & Cia (PASCUAL) San Sebastian, Spain and **BOOGAARD NV (BOOGAARD)** of Utrecht, Holland, conducted friendly discussions on a proposal for a joint undertaking to develop a Food Mixer (the **AB20**) and for a joint venture company (**PROCOL**) to manufacture **AB20** in Taiwan.

The parties have reached a tentative understanding, hereby sign this Letter of Preliminary Agreement (**LPA**) to establish clearly how they are willing to pursue.

1. AGREEMENTS

1.1 The parties will endeavour to conclude mutually acceptable Joint Venture Agreement, Technical Master Agreement and Distributor Agreement drafted and proposed by **PASCUAL** and the parties anticipate the need to obtain appropriate governmental approvals and shareholders' decisions.

1.2 In this purpose the parties agree that they will do their utmost to successfully assume their own responsibility stipulated in the attached "Working Guidelines" mutually agreed. It is agreed that the parties should undertake the following responsibilities:

2. RESPONSIBILITIES

2.1 * Engineering of **AB20** by **PASCUAL**
     * Prototype of **AB20** by **BOOGAARD**
     * Manufacturing Cost Analysis (Taiwan Simulation) of **AB20** by **BOOGAARD**
     * Business Plan of **PROCOL** by **PASCUAL/BOOGAARD**

3. DURATION

The parties agree that this **LPA** should be effective by October 31, 1993 and it is agreed that duration of this **LPA** can be extended by written consent of the parties.

4. COSTS

4.1 The parties agree that the costs they should bear to assume their responsibilities stipulated in Para. 2 shall remain in charge of each party without any claiming possibility in case of termination of LPA caused by any of the parties.

4.2 The parties agree that they should bear the costs for their responsibilities stipulated in Para. 2 and it is understood that the balance of costs born from the date of signature of this **LPA** between the parties could be amortised by Technical Master Agreement.

Select the best meaning from the alternatives given for the following words from the text on the previous page.

1 undertaking (line 2)   commitment/promise
             wish/need
             idea

2 hereby (5)   today
             near here
             by signing this document

3 pursue (6)   follow
             proceed
             develop

4 stipulated (12)   invented
             designed
             specified

5 effective (20)   useful
             in force
             good

6 consent (21)   permission
             idea
             letter

7 to assume responsibilities (23) to employ people
             to meet obligations
             to make money

8 bear (26)   refuse to pay costs
             increase costs
             meet costs

Text 3

Pre-reading

Many verbs have been removed from the paragraph on the opposite page. Complete the sentences with appropriate verbs. The first is already completed, as an example. If you have problems, look at the list of verbs which follows the exercise.

The parties (1) *enter into* an agreement to sell office equipment. According to the contract, the parties (2) .to work together for a minimum period of three years. Neither party is (3) . . . . to end the agreement without tendering written notice 90 days in advance. The contract, which is (4) . . . . 31st July 1991, (5) . . . . the responsibilities of each party. Either party is (6) . . . . .to sell the products in any state of South or Central America. The manufacturer shall (7) . . . . the distributor with all relevant documentation. if either party (8) . . . . on any item herein, the other shall have the right to (9) . . . . the agreement. In such circumstances, the terminating party should (10) . . . . the other party of its intention at least 90 days prior to the date intended for the termination. The terminating party should also (11) . . . . the reasons for the termination.

to be allowed	to terminate	to state
to be entitled	to furnish	to default
to be effective from	to undertake	to specify
	to notify	to enter into

Look at the text on the following page, and answer the following five questions.

1 What is the extract from?
2 What is the purpose of the document?
3 What companies are involved?
4 Which part of the document deals with advertising?
5 How is the document organised?

Distribution Agreement

This agreement is made and entered into on October 13th 1993, by and between Pohl Litbarski (Deutschland) GmbH, having its registered office at Kassel, Germany, hereinafter referred to as POHL, on the one side, and Bunge Luft AB, having its registered office in Bunge, Sweden, hereinafter referred to as BUNGE LUFT, on the other side.

Article 1

Territory and products
Section 1.01 POHL hereby appoints BUNGE LUFT its exclusive distributor in Sweden and Norway, hereinafter referred to as the territory, for the sale of all POHL presently as well as in the future manufactured products such as reciprocating and screw compressors, compressor packages and pumps as well as accessories and spare parts related thereto, hereinafter referred to as the products.

Article 2

Legal situation of the distributor
Section 2.01 BUNGE LUFT will buy and sell the products in its own name and for its own account. It will act as an independent trader as regards both POHL and its customers.

Section 2.02 POHL undertakes to sell the products within the territory only to BUNGE LUFT and shall not appoint any other distributor or agent for the products in the territory.

Section 2.03 POHL undertakes to refer all customers within the territory, who are enquiring about the products, to BUNGE LUFT.

Section 2.04 BUNGE LUFT is entitled to sell the products in countries outside the territory. The same rights with regard to the territory apply for POHL's distributors and agents outside the territory.

Article 3

Prices and conditions of payment
Section 3.01 POHL shall sell the products to BUNGE LUFT according to the price- list issued by POHL and applicable to all European distributors of the Pohl Litbarski group and being effective by the time of acceptance of BUNGE LUFT's order, presently according to schedule C.

Section 3.02 POHL reserves the right to change its price list by giving written notice to BUNGE LUFT ninety (90) days in advance.

Section 3.03 Payment for the products purchased by BUNGE LUFT shall be made 20 per cent cash on delivery and 80 per cent by signed draft to be paid at sight ninety (90) days from delivery.

Article 4

Advertising and Sales
Section 4.01 POHL agrees to continuously offer to actively support advertising and . . .

Scan the text on the previous page to find the following information.

1 What are the precise details of how Bunge Luft will get the products from Pohl and pay for them?
2 How can Pohl alter its prices?
3 Can other buyers of Pohl products sell them in Norway?
4 Does Pohl charge Bunge Luft higher prices than distributors in Southern Europe?

Transfer

Find a legal contract or other legal document that you are concerned with in your work. Apply some of the skills practised in this unit to find the following information.

• the subject of the document
• the parties involved
• the main obligations of each party
• the length of time the stipulations in the document are valid
• examples of potential conflict referred to in the document
• ways in which conflict can be resolved

Look again at the word list at the beginning of this unit. See if there are examples of any of these words in the document you have selected.

Note: If you are not concerned with any legal contract similar to those used in this unit, or have difficulty finding a copy, look instead at an insurance contract.

Answer Key

unit 1

1) *In Print*, Unit 1 Introductory Unit (the title of Chapter 1).
2) *The Australian Telecom Dream* (the heading of an article, p.6.
3) Everything between 'There is never . . .' and . . .'from what you read', p.1, the second paragraph in Unit 1.
4) The breakdown of sales and operating income by product group presented in two columns Sales/Operating Income as part of the Akzo text on p.5.
5) Unit 1 Introductory Unit pp. 1-13 is a chapter.
6) See p. *iii*.
7) This book does not have an Index. An index is an alphabetical list of topics, names of places or people mentioned in the book with page numbers indicating where each entry can be found. In British publications it is usually at the back of the book.
8) There is a diagram on p.41 as part of the introduction to the article on linking computer equipment.
9) Everything between the heading 'Introduction' on p.*iv* and the words 'presentations, discussions and meetings' is the Teacher's Introduction. The first paragraph of Unit Four, p.32 constitutes an introduction to the chapter. The bold print paragraph beginning 'The Australian telecom dream' on p.6 is the introduction to an article.
10) This book has no formal conclusion. Many books do have one, often in a chapter called 'Conclusion'. Reports frequently have 'Conclusions', see the last two paragraphs of the article on p.8, headed 'Conclusion and recommendations'. No chapter in this book has a formal conclusion either. Often the last paragraph in an article contains important information typical of a conclusion. See the examples on p.5 and p.9.

Task 2

The title of the article is Environment: *How green is your company?* on page 24. Possibly the article under the heading *Management Training* on page 35 would also be of interest.

Task 3

Pharmaceuticals Higher sales due to acquisitions (companies bought) in 1985.
Consumer products Sales were lower due to divestiture (sale) of Romi (oils and fats).

Task 4

1) a, c, e,   4) a, e
2) c, h   5) a
3) e

Task 5

1) True   4) False
2) False   5) True
3) False

The main point of the report is in the last sentence: 'The "European car" image is a positive one, and could become the basis for a distinct competitive advantage as car manufacturing and marketing become ever more global'.

Task 6

d) Yamaha selling high quality, cheaper saxophones.
e) Selmer reaching limit in American market – big effort outside America, Japan accounts for 20% of sales.
f) Labour cost is a big worry.

Task 7

1) there are some major differences . . .
2) To begin with, . . .
3) First, . . . Then . . . Finally, ...
4) But unlike . . .
5) For example, . . .
6) In the next lesson . . .
7) For now, . . .

Task 8

The most important information is that London needs more runways.

a) refers to the Air Transport User's Committee (in the first paragraph).
b) refers to Schiphol and Charles de Gaulle.
c) refers to Charles de Gaulle.

Task 9

1) a   3) c
2) c   4) b

unit 2

Task 1

1) use; computer printout showing series of rows and columns for doing accounts, calculations, etc.
2) instruction to computer by pressing specific keys on keyboard.
3) list of options available.
4) special word or combination of characters, personal to the user. It allows entry to computer system.
5) remove.
6) symbol showing the system is ready to receive a command.
7) list of files; sections of data held in memory.
8) recover, get back; (logged out = exited).
9) visuals e.g. pictures, charts, tables, graphs; a diagram showing comparison between two or more variables shown on two axes, the y (vertical) axis and the x (horizontal) axis.
10) look at alternatives.

Task 2

1) d   4) b
2) e   5) c
3) a

Task 3

all four

Task 4

1) c   3) d
2) a   4) b

Task 5

a) rows
b) columns
c) cell
d) cell pointer
e) window
f) scroll

Task 6

1) c
2) a
3) b

Task 7

a) Display
b) menu
c) Select
d) cursor
e) Enter
f) file
g) disk

Task 8

1) e   5) b
2) g   6) d
3) c   7) f
4) a

Task 9

1) Delete a password by selecting/File Save.
2) When the prompt appears, erase [PASSWORD PROTECTED] by pressing the Backspace or Esc key.
3) Press Enter to save the file.
4) After you have deleted [PASSWORD PROTECTED], press the space bar, type **p** and press Enter. Then enter and verify the new password.

unit 3

Task 1

1) prospect
2) market sector/segment
3) file
4) sales person
5) business card
6) competitor
7) client
8) sales force

Task 2

Prospecting is looking for, or identifying possible customers (prospects).

Task 3

Probably the best heading is c, then b, then a.

Task 4

A – 2 Prime prospect selection
B – 4 Customer acquisition
C – 1 Canvassing
D – 3 Hot prospects

Task 5

1) c
2) f
3) e
4) a
5) h
6) d
7) b
8) g

Task 6

1) True
2) False
3) False
4) True
5) False

Task 7

a) 2
b) 5
c) 1
d) 4
e) 3

Task 8

1) success – to succeed – successful
2) competitor, competition – to compete – competitive
3) payment, payee – to pay – paid
4) use – to use – useful
5) promotion, promoter – to promote – promotional
6) information, informer – to inform – informative
7) manufacturer, manufacturing – to manufacture – manufactured
8) value, valuer, valuation – to value – valuable
9) relation, relationship – to relate – relative, related
10) analysis – to analyse – analytical

Task 9

Summary 2

Task 10

a) 2
b) 4
c) 1
d) 3
e) 5

Task 11

1) Product promotion is activity designed to increase public awareness of products, their appeal and therefore sales. Such activity includes advertising, sponsorship (e.g. of sports, arts), sales promotion through special offers, etc.
2) By means of surveys, research, and other tests on market awareness of and opinion of a product.

Task 12

Public relations, sponsorship, sales promotion and advertising.

Task 13

a) Create
b) Make
c) Sell
d) Change
e) Inform
f) Retain
g) Build
h) Increase
i) Upgrade
j) Reduce

creation/sale/change/information/retention/
building*/increase/upgrade/reduction. * building (*n*)
is used only in the sense of a construction, e.g. a house,
part of a factory, warehouse, etc.

unit 4

Task 1

1) verifiable
2) to analyse
3) to profile
4) audit or survey
5) positioning
6) prospect(s)
7) cost-effective
8) to promote

Task 2

Probably both fact and opinion; he will justify opinion by describing experiences at Saab-Scania.

Task 3

4) The advertising business concentrates on advertisements and commercials.
5) No consistency so no clear Saab identity.
6) Our objective is to create a consistent message for all media.
7) Within this, we allow freedom for importers and agencies.
8) Advertising agencies do not like advertisers' involvement – they are increasingly criticised by advertisers. All these main points are opinion.

Task 4

1) He is very critical.
2) Saab has used surveys (para. 6) to show that their target group has similar preferences in all markets. He also refers to experience: 5/6 years ago agencies did not reply to their ideas; he also refers to other industries' criticisms of agencies.

Text 2 Pre-reading >M<

An agency that is able to provide all these advantages is probably very expensive and may even cost more than using various suppliers or employing own staff. Depending on the sector involved, few agencies would have really detailed knowledge of domestic and international markets. Many agencies may not, in reality, offer independent or objective opinions.
A possible order for the stated advantages is as follows: 5 2 3 4 6 1 7

Task 5

Hobson is expressing his opinion.

Task 6

1) Advantages: expertise in services; creative ability; experience of media; good technicians; good co-ordination of campaigns; agency package is convenient (easy all-in-one solution); agency sees proposition (the product and its advertising) from viewpoint of the market; agency is objective.
2) No, Hobson is very positive about advertising agencies.

Task 7

a) most convenient method;
b) manufacturer;
c) may not have independence to change management's decisions;
d) may not have experience of an agency.

Task 8

it – marketing strategy
who – larger concerns
they – larger concerns

Task 9

2 *manufacturer's* → his
3 *The manufacturer* → he
4 *the manufacturer's marketing position* → it
  the manufacturer's → his
8 *Looking at the same proposition from the market upwards* → this
10 *the manufacturer's personnel* → they

Task 10

Suggestions: marketing plans and changes should be based on verifiable data; use the last 5 years' data; use forecasts and published data to predict customer and market behaviour; forecast at 'current prices'.

Task 11

1) that can be checked/demonstrated
2) actions
3) predict
4) prediction(s)
5) accurate/good
6) expansion/development
7) strength/stature
8) needs
9) small groups of invited possible/typical customers
10) to judge
11) rarely

unit 5

Task 1

1) combination of equipment is not possible; any machinery for specific work; connecting.
2) positive characteristic (in a comparison); product which is a copy of an original version.
3) making everything compatible/able to work in combination; advantages.
4) advisers who are not employees; large combination of computers and terminals connected to a central computer.
5) disadvantage, negative point; machine attached to a computer for writing on paper; terminal, point where user of a computer system sits and works.
6) multiply, increase in number; to check.

Task 2 >M<

1) Integration produces efficiency, economy, technological benefits, easier access to information.
2) Difficult because of problems of compatibility between different software and hardware.
3) Processing speed, printing capabilities, age of equipment, type of processor, programming language, software, etc.
4) Creating networks, integration of computer equipment, advantages for business. The picture represents a network.

Task 3

1) e
2) a
3) d
4) b
5) c

From the first lines, we can say that the five paragraphs are probably about:

1) integration of microcomputers
2) benefits of linking
3) more benefits
4) integration is not easy
5) linking is complex

Task 4

benefits	= advantages
input	= to put in, to key in data
enables	= makes possible
carried out	= performed, done
workloads	= amount of work or

	business
processing speed	= speed at which the computer works
aiming	= with the intention of
share	= have
access	= entry
purchased	= bought

Task 5

1) Advantages include: users can work on same data, less duplication of work, internal electronic mail, standard letters and documents.
2) Factors affecting integration: processing speed, screen size, compatibility with other terminals using different programs.

Task 6

The article talks about computing, the cost, hardware and software.

Task 7

The meaning of the headings:

1 checking and limiting the quantity of material or data that is printed on paper
2 how system memory is used
3 use of outside professional advice
4 creating uniformity and explanation of any costs
5 well planned removal or relocation of old equipment
6 how to choose/select programs to buy

1)	b	4)	f
2)	e	5)	a
3)	d		

Task 8 >M<

1 Companies should have centralised purchasing control and approved manufacturers.
2 Check mailing lists, use Email internally and print less.
3 Use outside advice i.e. consultants.
4 Choose carefully, buy clones if they are good enough; at least justify decisions to pay for the security and support of a top name.
5 Monitor equipment use and department needs.
6 Use tape recording of data for less important data – it is cheaper (and slower, but that is not so important for old or less important data). Fast disk storage is very expensive.

Task 9

assessing	=	judging, making a decision based on something
outdated	=	out of date, old-fashioned
spreadsheet	=	software for financial and economic planning, and results
vetted	=	checked
clone	=	new product based on older usually more expensive design
allowed	=	permitted
Email	=	electronic mail, messages or other information sent electronically
recipients	=	people who receive something

The memo on page 47 can be completed with the following words:

a) Email
b) outdated
c) spreadsheet
d) vetted
e) Assesing
f) clone
g) recipients
h) allowed

Task 10

1) interconnection = integration or linking
2) to buy more computers, to buy more terminals linked to a central computer or to create a network.

Task 11

The three alternatives are:
i) multi-user microcomputer and/or supermicro
ii) minicomputer
iii) network

Task 12

1) standalone computer
2) expensive
3) cheap
4) industry standards
5) limited number of users
6) over 100 users
7) own system and language
8) network
9 - Possible answers are: unlimited users, link to
11) individuals and to peripherals, connects departments, reduces waiting.
12) complex

unit 6

Task 1

2) turnover
3) to earn
4) expenses
5) a survey
6) tax
7) an appointment
8) venture

Task 2

c) Learning the hard way

Task 3

1) Cause: He didn't know the meaning of *fair* for the Japanese.
   Result: He created dissension.
2) Cause: Being in the U.S.A., and the absence of a group environment.
   Result: He almost suffered a nervous breakdown.
3) Cause: Being in Great Britain and unable to use direct language.
   Result: He asked for a transfer.

Task 4

promoted, promotion, promise – transfer – semiconductor – coordinate – intercultural, international – superior – subsidiary

Ill in this context means badly, poorly or inadequately.

Task 5

across the Atlantic – communication between offices – half-round – under water (boat) – above the speed of sound – work with – push forward

Task 6 >M<

abstract – binary – degrade – illegal, irrelevant, impossible, inexact – misunderstood – predict – antistatic – contradict – extract – microcomputer – postpone – review

Task 7

Gross	= before tax has been deducted
Net	= after tax has been deducted
Adjusted	= a notional figure which takes into account cost of living and makes salary comparison between different countries possible.

Task 8

1) UK
2) Spain
3) Belgium
4) Finland

Task 9

Examples of the types of useful information which could be found are: names of the survey and its publishers; size of companies surveyed

Task 10

1) b
2) c
3) a
4) e
5) d

Task 11

1, 3 and 6 are correct.

unit 7

Task 1

1) liberalisation
2) destinations
3) deals
4) monopoly
5) independent
6) schedules
7) discount
8) compulsory
9) restriction
10) itinerary
11) stopovers
12) merger

Task 2

1) S
2) D
3) D
4) S
5) S
6) D
7) S
8) S

Task 3

1) b
2) a
3) b
4) c
5) c

Task 4

The authors main message is that many flights are too expensive but the situation is improving.

1) London – Paris = 5 × London – New York, London – Athens = 2 × London – New York.
2) The main problems are a compulsory Saturday night stay, advance booking and limits on flights.
3) a) British Midland
   b) Ryanair
   c) Virgin Atlantic

Task 5

1) key
2) liberalisation
3) discount
4) trip
5) revenue
6) segregate
7) round-trip
8) surcharge

Task 6

48 destinations – 250–280 days of travel – target of 280 days – 80–90 hours in air/month (Ronchi) – 60–70 hours in air/month (pilots and crews) – 120 days of travel = absolute limit – $300,000 this year's travel expenses for Ronchi – Memorex Telex had operations in 27 countries – 150–200 days travel in normal year

Task 7

a) health
b) financial
c) physical
d) mental
e) family
f) heart problems
g) wife

Task 8

Do
limit yourself to carry-on luggage; sit in an aisle seat; near the front; in the no-smoking section work; drink plenty of liquids; use airport business centres; collect mail from the airport (hotel)

Don't
check baggage; buy duty-free; eat all the food offered; drink alcohol

Task 9

c) is not acceptable, because up-to-date information on connections is not held by companies and the New York connection takes six times as long as Atlanta (not four).

unit 8

Task 1

1) the beginning
2) One of the startling findings . . . . . . is
3) b)
4) *Other surprise findings* . . . (1. 8) and *we also found that* . . . in the middle column
5) The use of bullets (•) before each finding

Task 2

1) 845
2) nearly 40%
3) 33.3%
4) £ 340–2600
5) Lotus 1-2-3 and dBase II and III
6) 28.4% (or 50% by value)
7) 365 sites (about 40%).

Task 3

1) The standalone microcomputer is less popular than microcomputers that are connected to other machines.
2) Any five of the following:
   i. 'End user computing' will grow rapidly.
   ii. Many micros are already used for communicating with other machines.
   iii. Senior managers are the fastest growing category of new users.
   iv. The IBM PC standard is dominant.
   v. There are more connected microcomputers than expected.
   vi. The most used software is the spreadsheet.

Task 4

Country	System code	Start date	Run by	Target
Britain	IDA	???	British Telecom	???
Germany	ISDN	Jan 88	Deutsche Bundespost	600 exchanges by 1993
France	ISDN	Dec 87	France Telecom	95,000 users by 1992

The problems are:
a) delays and disagreements
b) little pressure from users for progress in developing ISDN

Task 5

for example (line 12) signals an example
however (line 19) introduces a contrast and is used as the first word in the sentence and is followed by a comma
although (line 27) also signals a contrast, but is used after a comma and is followed by a determiner (*these*)
Nevertheless (line 30) contrast, first word in the sentence. It means the same as 'Despite what you have just read in the previous sentence(s) . . .'
and (line 32) addition
however (line 34) contrast again. Here it means 'Yes, there are two exchanges using ISDN in Mannheim and Stuttgart, but in fact the true test of ISDN is coming with the full commercial service'
however (line 50) contrast. After hearing of successful applications of ISDN, now a problem is signalled by this use of however – at the end of a sentence. Note: this however could equally have occurred at the beginning of the sentence followed by a comma
but (line 52) also signals a contrast – more negative news

Task 6

1) but/although
2) and
3) Because
4) Although
5) however
6) if

Task 7

Program 1
1) Brainstorm
2) David Tebbut
3) ideas/text organiser
4) thought maps
5) breaking down large tasks into small tasks.

Program 2
1) Agenda
2) Lotus
3) flexible free-form database program
4) 'items', 'categories' and 'notes'
5) possible to type in text before setting up categories

Task 8

1)	f	4)	a
2)	d	5)	c
3)	e	6)	b

Task 9

Priorities: 1) decision support software
2) ISDN
Term: software – short/medium
ISDN – medium/long

unit 9

Task 1

output – industrial production
wholesale prices – cost of goods sold at factory
government spending – (also known as public spending) what government spends, government costs
capital investment – businesses' spending on machinery, equipment, etc
patent – product licence, licence to be the only producer of a product
GDP – annual value of goods and services sold in a country, including sales to other countries
demand – retail sales/consumption *consumption*-consumer spending (see **demand** above)
interest rates – cost of borrowing money
outlook – forecast for the future (same as **prospects**)
revenue – income
housebuilding – domestic construction/house construction
inflation – rising costs, prices and wages
growth – economic development, increased GDP
prospects – forecast for the future
manpower – number of people working in an industry

Task 2

1 a) -3.3   b) +10.9   c) 9.9   d) 10.2
2 a) Japan has better output, much higher demand and much lower unemployment than the U.S.A.
b) Japan's industrial production in the last three months much lower than in Germany; for the year, both have increased output (+ 3.5 in Japan, + 4.0 for Germany). Similar GDP; German demand much higher, Japanese unemployment much lower.

Task 3

1 a) + 4.9   b) + 4.9   c) + 3.2   d) + 6.3
2 a) Similar rises in prices, but the U.S. has higher wholesale price increases. Wages are increasing more slowly in the U.S. than in Japan.
b) Similar rises in prices for Japan and Germany, but Germany has lower consumer price increases over 12 months. Wage rises are similar.

Task 4

1) As interest rates rise, housebuilding falls which signals a downturn in the economy. Later, increased housebuilding usually signals the recovery.
2) a) United States
b) Britain
c) Japan
3) Continuing fall in U.S. housebuilding; in Japan and Germany situation quite good – and same as previous year.

Task 5

to increase ↗	to rise ↗	to remain at →
to drop ↘	to fall ↘	to edge down ↘
to soar ↗	to touch bottom ↘	

2) to rise-rose-risen   to fall-fell-fallen
3) to edge down – to decrease just a little;
to soar – to increase very rapidly;
to touch bottom – to reach the lowest point
4) to increase (*v*) an increase (*n*); to rise (*v*) a rise (*n*); to drop (*v*) a drop (*n*); to fall (*v*) a fall (*n*).
5) The common words that could be included here are:
to grow, (grew, grown), growth (*n*)
to expand, expansion (*n*)
to go up
to climb, climb (*n*)
to decline, decline (*n*)
to go down
to stay the same
to stabilise
to level out, levelling out (*n*)

Task 6

The main message of the article is that Japan invests a lot in R&D and the economy benefits with a high share of patented products developed in Japan and a big share of world high tech products market. Finance is cheap in Japan, but R&D is a central priority.

Task 7

Para. 3	13% of revenue spent on R&D.
Para. 4	R&D is central. It is cheaper than in other countries.
Para. 5	R&D has been cheaper, maybe not now.
Para. 6	Other factors mean big spending on R&D (high growth, a lot of co-operation, helpful banks).
Para. 7	High speed growth, banks help.
Para. 8	Co-operation between companies.
Para. 9	Cost of capital has increased; other advantages remain.

Task 8

Factors having a positive effect on the economy	Factors with a potentially negative effect
high interest rates	tightening labour market
lower consumption	higher oil prices
fiscal restraint	
increased government surplus	
rise in the yen	
GNP has increased	

Task 9

1 a) inflation fears have grown;
   b) more restrictive monetary policy;
2 persistent labour shortages
3 a) fiscal restraint;
   b) demand may fall;
   c) unemployment may increase.

Task 10

2) prompted
3) due to
5) led to
6) result in
7) because of

Task 11

sustained by – a) buoyant – b) further – c) prompting – b) domestic demand – a) capacity utilisation – c) labour shortages – b) interest rates – b) fiscal restraint – c) surplus – b) thus – c) slightly – b) offset – c) appreciation – a)

Task 12

to grow – to increase, to develop
to rise – to go up, to increase
to remain high – same as to remain strong
to decelerate – same as to slow
to subside – to fall, to diminish, to lose strength
to expand – to increase, to develop
to rebound – to recover quickly after a fall
to remain unchanged – to stay the same
to decline – to fall, to go down
to remain strong – to stay at a good level
to slow – to reduce (the rate or speed of something)
to increase – to go up
to ease – to diminish, get smaller
to stagnate – to stay at a low level
to fall – to go down
to pick up – to recover

Task 13

1) No – similar to Germany, much better than the U.S.
2) Yes
3) Yes
4) Yes
5) Yes
6) No – 20.6%
7) Yes.

unit 10

Task 1

1) *dividend* - a quantity of money, being a percentage of profits, paid to shareholders.
   share - a part of the total capital of a company.
2) *lend* - to give for a period of time, after which the thing or the money is returned/the opposite of to borrow.
3) *loan* - a sum of money given for a period of time, i.e. lent.
   freehold land and buildings - any property owned or mortgaged, but not rented.
   assets - anything, including cash, of marketable value/that can be sold.
4) *liabilities* - debts/money owed.

Task 2

1) creditors
2) opening stock
3) balance sheet
4) profit & loss account
5) fixed assets
6) current assets
7) depreciation
8) cost of sales
9) shares/ordinary share capital

Task 3

1) abridged accounts of Pangloss to show what is used to judge the financial strength of a company
2) depreciation
3) interest

Task 4

The two elements are depreciation and interest. They are important because both are high and affect final pre-tax profit considerably.
Depreciation: trading surplus less depreciation = pre-interest profits – a very important figure; also perhaps because depreciation in this example is high.
Interest: high interest payments greatly reduce profits. Interest here is 30% of pre-interest profits; this is very high.
A 70% increase in sales + £1.7m, less interest (£0.3m) = $1.4m pre-tax profits – double present profits. A 70% decrease in sales + £0.3m, less interest (£0.3m) = £0.00, i.e., no profits. Potential lenders need to examine present sales performance and probable future sales performance. Only very good prospects could justify lending more money.

Task 5

1) They probably should not.
2) To examine trading (sales) prospects. It would probably be better to invest in gilts.

Task 6

1) investor	8) gross
2) reasonable	9) gilts
3) long-term	10) judge
4) net	11) trading prospects
5) deducted	12) prospects
6) standard	13) steadily
7) recipient	

Task 7

1) £5m
2) £11m

Task 8

1) no
2) probably not
3) probably not

Task 9

1) share capital – no. of shares = £3 (6m – 2m = 3).
2) £3m mortgage, £2m bank overdraft; £6m left.
3) potential for finding/borrowing more money.
4) the ability of the company to service the interest charge out of current profits, and asset backing for loans.
5) ability to pay interest charges/the cost of borrowing out of the profit the company is making.
6) amount of money, property, machinery etc that the company has and that can be used as security to guarantee loans.
7) interest payments of 4% on a loan (like a mortgage) to buy property
8) the loan has to be paid back (or renegotiated).
9) the company will probably need more funds to pay increased interest and mortgage repayments after the present debenture is renegotiated, probably at a much higher rate.

unit 11

Task 1

1) gross
2) cash flow
3) allocation
4) cash
5) demand
6) budget
7) raw materials
8) debtor
9) cost of sales (This term is also written as *cost of goods sold*).
Other definitions: *Commission* (noun) money paid to a salesman or agent, usually a percentage of the sales made. *Expenditure* (noun) amounts of money spent. *Liquidity* (noun) having cash or assets which can be changed into cash. *Net* (adj) price or weight or pay etc after all deductions have been made. *Overheads* (noun) money spent on the day-to-day cost of a business.

Profitability (noun) ability to make a profit. *Unit* (noun) single product for sale. *Variable* (noun) something which changes, or (adj) which changes. *Selling costs* (amount of money to be paid for advertising, reps' commissions, etc involved in selling something).

Task 2

1) c
2) b
3) f
4) e
5) g

Task 3

1) 56,000
2) £10.00
3) £12.50
4) £600,000
5) 5%
6) £23,000
7) £95,000
    All information from Tables 1 and 2.

Task 4

1) pricing policy
2) seasonal influences e.g., winter sales of ski equipment would be higher than spring/summer sales
3) total amount of non-regular business may be approximately the same every year
4) variety of expertise
5) different advertising costs, markets or incremental costs

Task 5

1) £594,000
2) direct labour
3) £609,500
4) £7,000

Task 6

1) Cash flow represents ability to pay dividends, to succeed and to grow in the future.
2) The cash budget helps management to plan, to avoid unwanted unproductive cash balances and to reduce expensive short-term borrowing.
3) One month.
4) One year.
5) No. Depreciation is not a cash item.

Task 7

1) debtors
2) creditors
3) liabilities
4) collections (this is in the table)
5) cash balances
6) short-term deficiencies
7) depreciation

Task 8

1) To judge if the financial position of the company is satisfactory: i.e., to examine profitability, liquidity (availability of cash) and financing.
2) It is static i.e., it shows expected results for only one level of sales, costs, etc. Also the cost of goods sold is only very approximate.
3) Allocated fixed costs + depreciation on fixed assets used in the production.

Task 9

1) £600,000
2) £180,000
3) £160,000
4) £20,000
5) £335,000
6) opening value of assets £260,000; capital additions £25,000; less depreciation £10,000; total £285,000

unit 12

Task 1

1) to start a partnership/collaboration
2) stated/said
3) according to the document/contract; only/exclusively; advance agreement/permission
4) breaking of the agreement/breach of contract by; would have the right to
5) present a complaint (through a solicitor/lawyer); saying there has been; operative
6) said; change
7) people/companies involved in a contract
8) promise

Task 2

1) the introduction
2) a proposal to work together in a partnership (on a specific project) a joint venture agreement
3) para 1 introduces the companies involved; para 2 states relationship of 'F' to the product; para 3 states purpose/intention of the agreement.

Task 3

this → the agreement; **this** → the day/date; **'F'** → Fornaro; **its** – Warwick Photographic; **'W'** → Warwick Photographic; **'F'** → Fornaro; **the parties** → Fornaro and Warwick Photographic; **such** → the designing, manufacturing, assembling and marketing of the JWS-20; **them** → Fornaro and Warwick Photographic; **said** → the designing, manufacturing, assembling and marketing of the JWS-20; **their** → Fornaro and Warwick Photographic; **products** → JWS-20.

Task 4

1) to establish the basis for a joint venture.
2) Pascual Ruiz Cabestany & Cia, Boogaard NV.
3) food mixer AB20.
4) not stated, but can be extended by mutual agreement.
5) engineering by Pascual; prototype, manufacturing cost analysis by Boogaard; both parties to design business plan.
6) each party pays costs for its responsibilities; other costs amortised by Technical Master Agreement.

Task 5

1) promise
2) by signing this document
3) follow
4) specified
5) in force
6) permission
7) to meet obligations
8) meets costs

Task 6

2) undertake
3) allowed
4) effective from
5) states
6) entitled
7) furnish
8) defaults
9) terminate
10) notify
11) specify

Task 7

1) The extract is from a distribution agreement.
2) It states the conditions which apply to the agreement in terms of territory, obligations, prices, conditions of payment, advertising details, etc of the parties involved.
3) The agreement is between Pohl Litbarski GmbH and Bunge Luft.
4) Article 4 deals with advertising.
5) It is organised into articles and sections.

Task 8

1) It will buy the products direct from Pohl at prices issued by them. Payment will be 20% on delivery and 80% by signed draft 90 days later.
2) By writing to Bunge Luft giving 90 days notice of the price increase.
3) Yes.
4) No.